GH00991999

40 D

WITH PAUL

BOOT
CAMP

READ

LEARN

THINK

PRAY

A JOURNEY THAT COULD CHANGE YOUR WORLD

MISSION CO-ORDINATOR:

DOMINIC

SMART

BOOT
CAMP

READ

LEARN

THINK

PRAY

BLYTHSWOOD CARE

CF4•K

10 9 8 7 6 5 4 3 2 1

40 Days with Paul

© Dominic Smart 2010

ISBN 978-1-84550-567-7

Boot Camp and other extra features © Christian Focus Publications

Published by Christian Focus Publications

Geanies House, Fearn, Tain, Ross-shire,

IV20 1TW, Scotland, UK.

www.christianfocus.com

Cover design: MOOSE77.COM

Printed and bound by Bell and Bain, Glasgow

CF4•K
*Because you're never
too young to know Jesus*

2 CORINTHIANS 4:6-7

For God, who said, "Let light shine out of
darkness," made his light shine in our hearts to
give us the light of the knowledge of the glory
of God in the face of Christ. But we have this
treasure in jars of clay to show that this all-
surpassing power is from God and not from us.

BLYTHSWOOD CARE

MISSION AND TASK

For the next 40 days your mission is to read through the scriptures that focus on Paul's life and writings in order to find out what God is saying to you.

READ

BIBLE READINGS
Location: pages 16–106.
Description: Read through Acts, the Epistles and other related scriptures.

LEARN

THINK ABOUT IT
Location: pages 16–106.
Description: What Paul's life and writings teach us.

THINK

THINK SPOTS
Location: At different points throughout the book.
Description: Extra information.

PRAY

READ THIS AND PRAY
Location: At the end of each reading.
Description: A Bible verse and brief prayer to God.

RESEARCH FACILITY

WORDS

BOOT CAMP

Further information about words and concepts highlighted in the book.

WORDS
Root out the meanings of certain words on Location: pages 109-113.

BOOT CAMP
If you feel ready you can start the Mission by turning straight to page 14. However some of us will need a bit of help to get started so you can go over some of the basics in the Boot Camp section at the back of the book. These are lessons that can help you get to grips with some information before you start the main lessons.
Location: page 116-122.
Description: Initiation for the 40 days task.

MAPS

WHO'S WHO

MAPS
See where it all took place on our Mission Maps.
Location: page 126-127.

WHO'S WHO
A summary of the key characters.
Location: page 114.

Turn the page to read
the mission statement
from Dominic Smart.

Your Mission – should you choose to accept it is to...

READ ABOUT THE LIFE OF PAUL AND HIS WRITINGS IN 40 DAYS

Dear Friend,

We are all on a journey through life. When we follow Jesus we travel through life on the route that he maps out for us.

So what kind of journey does Jesus take his followers on? Well, it's a missionary journey. Every one of his followers is on his mission. And his mission is to reach the world with the good news of God's saving love and to create a people who will be like him in their love for God and their love for one another. That's the mission of God. There will be new days only as long as God's mission is unfinished. Once it's finished, Jesus will return and the end of this world will come.

That means you have a purpose in life and there's a reason today is happening. There's a call and a commission from the King of all creation that is just for you and for all who follow Jesus. If you're a Christian you're on a mission with God: simple as that!

In the Bible we are shown a remarkable man who lived the mission. He was born Saul but when he began to follow Jesus his name changed to Paul. He wrote a lot of our New Testament; he spent much of his life on missionary journeys; he had some really difficult times and some wonderfully happy times; he always travelled with friends – sometimes they fell out, but they loved one another just the same.

We can learn so much from Paul. So the next forty days are part of the training for the rest of the mission – the rest of your life as a follower of Jesus.

We'll track Paul's life from the time when he became a Christian. Each day we will think about verses from the Book of Acts or from other parts of the New Testament as we go with Paul on his journeys round the Mediterranean with the gospel. We start though with the personal journey that Paul had to make before he could start out with God on God's mission.

One final thing: I've been on this mission with God for over thirty-six years and I want you to know that there hasn't been a day when Jesus has not been the most wonderful friend and companion. He's picked me up when I've been down, guided me to where I should be, forgiven me when I've messed up, trained me when I didn't know what to do or think. He's given me some great teachers and friends and has constantly supplied what I've needed. It hasn't always been easy but the most difficult days have been the ones I've learned most about his love.

So if you haven't begun this journey yet, don't delay. If you have, don't give up!

Your friend,

Dominic

Mission Co-ordinator data file: Turn to page 8
Accept your mission: Turn to page 9
Bible Readings and Topics: Turn to page 10
Brush up with a boot camp before you get started: Turn to page 116.
Check out the maps: Turn to page 126-127.

MISSION CO-ORDINATOR – DOMINIC SMART.

PLACE OF BIRTH:

Dominic Smart was born in Yorkshire, but has lived in Scotland for the past thirty years.

PRESENT SITUATION:

He is the Minister of Gilcomston South Church in the centre of Aberdeen. He is a regular speaker at conferences and universities and is a visiting lecturer at the Highland Theological College.

FAMILY LIFE:

Dominic and his wife, Marjorie, have three daughters and a son. They also have a couple of pets: two cats and a Springer Spaniel.

SPARE TIME:

Dominic likes jazz music, films, Indian food and proper coffee but can't get enough of any of them; the nearest thing to a hobby is trying to catch up on sleep.

CHRISTIAN LIFE:

He became a Christian in 1973 after an Arthur Blessitt meeting in Bradford City football ground, and for many years was involved in United Beach Missions. He has written several books, including *When We Get It Wrong*, on failure; *Grace, Faith and Glory*, on the Bible's antidotes to legalism; and *Kingdom Builders*, on Peter, Stephen and Philip in Acts.

STRANGE BUT TRUE:

Dominic would like to change two things about himself – everything he does and everything he says. But even then it would probably be wrong! His only really embarrassing moment was genuinely too embarrassing to tell in public.

MISSION ACCEPTED?

Yes! In the next 40 Days I want
to read about the Apostle Paul
and the mission of Jesus Christ
that could change my world.

Signed:

....

Date:

....

BIBLE READINGS AND TOPICS

PART 3 REFER TO ACTS 13 & 14
THE FIRST JOURNEY: PAUL IS ON A MISSION
— YOU'RE ON IT TOO!

PAGE 40-57

PART 4 ACTS 15:36-41
PAUL IS ONLY HUMAN: SO ARE YOU!

PAGE 58-67

PART 5 ACTS 15:40 – 18:22
PAUL'S SECOND MISSIONARY JOURNEY:
YOUR HEART AND GOD'S MISSION

PAGE 68-81

PART 6 ACTS 18:23 – 20:38
PAUL'S THIRD JOURNEY:
HOW TO STRENGTHEN OTHER BELIEVERS

PAGE 82-93

Part 7 Acts 21:17 – 28:31
Paul's Fourth Journey: Be faithful to God all the way

Page 94-107

35. Luke 12:4-12 & 22-26, Arrested in Caesarea:
     Jesus keeps his promises

36. Acts 26:28-32, Before wicked leaders:
     Some people couldn't care less!

37. Acts 27:21-26, All at sea: Being a leader in a crisis

38. Acts 28:11-14, Safe arrival: Who gets you through
     life's journeys?

39. Acts 28:30-31, Colossians 4:2-5, Paul in Rome:
     Never stop serving God

40. 2 Timothy 3:10-17, Top tips for missionaries

Part 1

God turns Saul into Paul

Before we are sent out on God's mission we need the life-changing work of God in our own lives. We can know about God, we can believe that there is a God, we can even live a (good) life, but still not be a Christian.

Paul knew all about God from the Old Testament. He could recite the scriptures, he certainly believed in the God who had revealed himself in the Old Testament and he tried to live a good life. But he wasn't in a right relationship with God.

Paul had two major problems: he didn't believe that Jesus was God's Saviour and King, the Messiah; and he thought that the way to get right with God was by doing all the right things according to God's law, rather than by faith in God's grace. He wasn't alone in this. He had learned it from devout Jews and many good people believed the same thing.

Saul of Tarsus had to be converted before he could be Paul, the missionary. He had to be changed, heart, soul and mind. And so do we. God had to work in Saul before he could work through Saul. Saul had to stop working against God before he could work with God.

Over the next few days we will see how God did the converting work in Saul. Ask God to make it very clear to you if you need the same work too.

Words: grace; believe; mission; Saviour – pages 109-113
Boot Camp 005/The Old Testament – page 121

SECTION 1
ACTS 9:1-19
GOD TURNS SAUL INTO PAUL

DAY 1 BIBLE READING

ACTS 9:1-2 – SAUL'S CONVERSION

¹Meanwhile, Saul was still breathing out murderous threats against the Lord's disciples. He went to the high priest ²and asked him for letters to the synagogues in Damascus, so that if he found any there who belonged to the Way, whether men or women, he might take them as prisoners to Jerusalem.

READ THIS: He who is not with me is against me (Matthew 12:18).

THINK ABOUT THIS: Many people have tried to wipe the name of Jesus from the history books. Can you think of some famous people who have tried to do away with God? Some have tried to kill and hurt Christ's followers. Some have written books in order to deceive people. Where are most of these people now? Death comes to all of us, but, no matter who is against God, God is never defeated. He is eternal. "If God is for us, who can be against us?" (Romans 8:31)

THINK ABOUT IT: DAY 1 ACTS 9:1-2
GOD'S ENEMY

Our first day with Paul isn't a good one. As Saul of Tarsus he has decided to be an enemy of God's infant Church because he wants to wipe the name of Jesus from the history books. Jesus was very blunt when he said that we are all either for him or against him: there's no fence to sit on, no neutrality about his place in our lives. We've either yielded our lives to the one and only Saviour or we haven't. Saul had his own way of being right with God and his own ideas of what God is like – none of it included Jesus.

So Saul set off to Damascus to try and wipe out the Church that worshipped Jesus and that told people about the gospel of God's wonderful Saviour. But God is bigger than Saul and God wanted to send Saul out to tell people the gospel. So first Saul had to be converted. And if God can save Saul, he can save you.

READ THIS AND PRAY: And we have seen and testify that the Father has sent his Son to be the Saviour of the world (1 John 4:14).

Prayer: Heavenly Father, forgive me if I have not yet trusted Jesus as the only Saviour that you have given to the world. Forgive me if deep in my heart I am in fact your enemy. Help me now to trust your Son, Jesus, and to accept him as my only Saviour and Lord. Amen.

Words: converted; eternal; Father; gospel; Saviour; – pages 109-113
Maps: Damascus – see page 126

DAY 2 BIBLE READING
Acts 9:3-4 – Saul's Conversion

³As he neared Damascus on his journey, suddenly a light from heaven flashed around him. ⁴He fell to the ground and heard a voice say to him, "Saul, Saul, why do you persecute me?"

CHURCH: The term 'the Church' is the name used to describe the group of people who worship the Lord Jesus Christ as their Saviour. It is a word that is also used to describe the building in which Christians generally worship. Believers and their families meet together as the Church of Christ to learn from God's Word, pray to their heavenly Father and praise him. The Church belongs to Christ and today it is growing across the world – even in countries where believers are persecuted for following Jesus.

SIN: Sin is doing, saying or thinking anything that is against God's commands. It is also not doing, saying and thinking what God has commanded. Sin is missing the mark that God has set. God has set a perfect standard. When we fail to live up to that perfect standard in the smallest way that is sin. God cannot abide sin in his presence. That is why the consequence of sin is death to all who do not trust in Jesus Christ. The only remedy for sin is to trust in Jesus Christ's death on the cross. His death is the only power to defeat sin. Forgiveness for sin is only available through Christ's sacrifice on the cross.

THINK ABOUT IT: DAY 2   ACTS 9:3-4
JESUS AND YOU: IT'S PERSONAL

It's important to see how personally Jesus takes Saul's hatred of the Church. It means two things: that Jesus' friends are very special to him – what hurts them hurts him. It also means that people never simply reject ideas or teaching about Jesus – it's him that they are saying no to.

Sin is always a big fat 'No!' to Jesus personally. It says 'No!' to his way of living. It says 'My way is better, thank you!' And it says 'No!' to what Jesus has done for sinners on the cross. People never simply say 'No!' to the Christian religion; they say 'No!' to a relationship with Christ.

Jesus had to confront Saul about all this. Sooner or later he will confront everyone about it. If we spend our life saying 'No!' to Jesus he will turn to us in the end and say 'OK, have it that way then.' And he will say 'No!' to us. How much better to get on good terms with Jesus now.

READ THIS AND PRAY: This is the confidence we have in approaching God: that if we ask anything according to his will, he hears us. And if we know that he hears us— whatever we ask—we know that we have what we asked of him (1 John 5:14-15).

Prayer: Heavenly Father, help me to see clearly that it is my relationship with Jesus Christ that is of primary importance. Help me to see it that way when I think of my friends and my family too. Thank you so much that Jesus wants me and them to be his friends forever. Amen.

Boot Camp 001/Sin & Punishment – page 116
Boot Camp 004/Creation & the Fall – page 120

DAY 3 BIBLE READING
COLOSSIANS 1:21-22

21Once you were alienated from God and were enemies in your minds because of your evil behaviour. 22But now he has reconciled you by Christ's physical body through death to present you holy in his sight, without blemish and free from accusation.

CREATION: To find out about how our world was made read Genesis 1–3. God made all living things with the ability to reproduce so he is not only the Creator of the first creatures or the first man and woman. He is the Creator of all living things and all mankind.

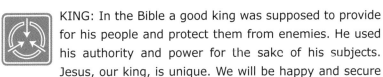

KING: In the Bible a good king was supposed to provide for his people and protect them from enemies. He used his authority and power for the sake of his subjects. Jesus, our king, is unique. We will be happy and secure if we serve and obey him. He governs us faithfully and wants our good. He even left heaven for a time to live among us. He died to purchase his followers a place in heaven, but especially when they leave this world at death. Then they will go to heaven to share and enjoy it with him. If Jesus is your king then you should help others, in his name, as he helps you.

THINK ABOUT IT: DAY 3
COLOSSIANS 1:21-22
JESUS CANNOT BE IGNORED

Everyone of us – including Saul – has a relationship with Jesus. We can't escape a relationship with Jesus because of two things about him. First, he is our Maker. Just because Saul denied who Jesus was doesn't mean that Jesus didn't make Saul. Many of us might not know who our parents are, but we certainly had parents! The other thing about Jesus is that he is Lord of all things. If I say that he doesn't exist it doesn't make Jesus get off the throne and disappear in a puff of smoke.

Saul lived a lie. The lie was that Jesus had nothing to do with Saul. On the road to Damascus the lie was blown to pieces as the Creator and King stopped Saul in his rebellious tracks. The amazing thing is that Jesus did so because he loved Saul and wanted Saul to follow him on his great mission in the world.

Everyone you meet today is in the same situation. What kind of a relationship do they – and you – have with Jesus? Rebel or follower?

READ THIS AND PRAY: Remember your Creator in the days of your youth, before the days of trouble come (Ecclesiastes 12:1).

Prayer: Lord Jesus, thank you that you made me and are the loving Lord. I acknowledge you to be my Maker and my Lord. Help me to follow you all the days of my life, starting today. Amen.

Words: Creator – page 109

Boot Camp 002/Getting started with God – page 117
Boot Camp 003/Introducing Jesus – page 118

DAY 4 BIBLE READING

ACTS 9:15-16

[15]But the Lord said to Ananias, "Go! This man is my chosen instrument to carry my name before the Gentiles and their kings and before the people of Israel. [16]I will show him how much he must suffer for my name."

SIN. We have to have our sin dealt with. Sin is a problem. Jesus deals with the problem. One of the ways to explain how he does this is by using the word 'covering'. He takes his goodness and covers our badness with it. When God looks at us he sees Jesus' goodness. Our sin is no longer there. All our sin is covered. This is not Jesus pretending to God the Father in order to trick him. God the Father is fully aware of what is happening. He has planned it all.

YOUR LIFE: How can the way that you do things today show people what God is like so that they might turn to him?

THINK ABOUT IT: DAY 4 ACTS 9:15-16
JESUS HAS A MISSION FOR YOU

Does Jesus save Saul from his sin just for Saul's sake?

Actually, no. Part of the reason why God saves us is that we can glorify him with everything that we do. He saves us partly (in fact, mostly) for his own sake. Glorifying him is the best thing for us to do so we benefit as well!

Jesus has work for Saul to join in with. It's work that the Father and the Spirit are doing with Jesus, and now they want Saul to join in. There are two wonderful lessons here for you. First, God gives you a purpose in life. Second, God can take his most violent enemies and turn their relationship with him around so that they glorify him.

God's mission for you is the same that Saul was given – share in God's mission to glorify himself in all the earth. Share the good news about Jesus with others, live a transformed life, give glory to God with everything you do. What a mission!

READ THIS AND PRAY: Whoever serves me must follow me; and where I am, my servant also will be. My Father will honour the one who serves me (John 12:26).

It is the Lord Christ you are serving (Colossians 3:24).

Prayer: Lord Jesus, thank you that you give me a reason to live that outlasts any other. Help me to be about your work today. Amen.

Words: glorify; mission; sin (also see pages 18 and 22); see pages 109-113

DAY 5 BIBLE READING
Acts 9:10-16

[10]In Damascus there was a disciple named Ananias. The Lord called to him in a vision, "Ananias!"

"Yes, Lord," he answered.

[11]The Lord told him, "Go to the house of Judas on Straight Street and ask for a man from Tarsus named Saul, for he is praying. [12]In a vision he has seen a man named Ananias come and place his hands on him to restore his sight."

[13]"Lord," Ananias answered, "I have heard many reports about this man and all the harm he has done to your saints in Jerusalem. [14]And he has come here with authority from the chief priests to arrest all who call on your name."

[15]But the Lord said to Ananias, "Go! This man is my chosen instrument to carry my name before the Gentiles and their kings and before the people of Israel. [16]I will show him how much he must suffer for my name."

WORLDLY WISDOM: The Bible says that God's ways and thoughts are not like ours (Isaiah 55:8). Worldly wisdom is when human beings think their own thoughts and plans without following God or even taking his views into account. That's not wise at all.

STRENGTH FOR THE MISSION: If we need the Holy Spirit then it means that we can't do God's work in our own strength or rely on the world's wisdom. So today and every day, as you go on God's mission, ask for his strengthen and wisdom. He will give you both through the Holy Spirit who lives in you.

THINK ABOUT IT: DAY 5 – ACTS 9:10-16 JESUS SENDS THE HOLY SPIRIT – YOU'RE NEVER ALONE!

So Saul is a changed man with a new purpose in life. But he can't really do the work of God's mission without God's power and guidance. So God sends the Holy Spirit to him through Ananias so that Saul can do what God calls him to do and join in Jesus' great mission.

A short while before Jesus met Saul, Jesus had sent the disciples out on the same mission. They had to wait until they too received the Spirit or 'power from on high' as Jesus had said in Luke 24:49; 'You will receive power' was what he said in Acts 1:8.

That's good news! It means that God is always with us to give us everything that we need for his mission. He doesn't give you a task then watch from a distance. He's with you. And he is with you in order to give you the power that you need. You're never alone on God's mission!

 READ THIS AND PRAY: If any of you lacks wisdom, he should ask God, who gives generously to all without finding fault, and it will be given to him (James 1:5).

But the wisdom that comes from heaven is first of all pure; then peace-loving, considerate, submissive, full of mercy and good fruit, impartial and sincere (James 3:17).

Prayer: Thank you, Lord God, for the power that you give your people. You have not left me alone to complete the task. You have given me a mission to do for your kingdom but I need not worry as you will be my ever present help. Amen.

Who's Who: Holy Spirit – page 115
Words: Mercy; Wisdom – see pages 109-113
Maps: Jerusalem; Damascus – see pages 126-127

DAY 6 BIBLE READING
ACTS 9:17-19

[17]Then Ananias went to the house and entered it. Placing his hands on Saul, he said, "Brother Saul, the Lord—Jesus, who appeared to you on the road as you were coming here—has sent me so that you may see again and be filled with the Holy Spirit." [18]Immediately, something like scales fell from Saul's eyes, and he could see again. He got up and was baptized, [19]and after taking some food, he regained his strength.

EARTHLY GLORY: When we think about Jesus and focus on God's Word, when we long to please our Heavenly Father more than any other person, then we are focussing more on heaven and God's glory than on temporary earthly glory. We are becoming more like Christ.

EARTHLY FEARS: These are the fears that we have about life and death, the concerns we have about what we are going to drink, eat, wear. The Bible tells us, however, that we are not to worry about these things. God provides for the lilies and the sparrows. Sparrows are of very little value when sold in a market but not one of them falls to the ground without God knowing about it. We are of much more value than a sparrow. Every hair of your head is numbered by the Lord. He loves and will provide for your needs.

**THINK ABOUT IT: DAY 6   ACTS 9:17-19
JESUS GIVES YOU HELPERS**

God put Ananias in Damascus. God spoke to Ananias and sent him to Saul. Ananias was a huge blessing to Saul, a good new friend.

Ananias was afraid of what Saul had come to Damascus to do. Saul had been the enemy of the Church, a paid assassin. But Ananias still said 'Yes' to God. God's plan for Saul would have seemed really strange to Ananias, but he still went to see him. He had a willing heart that would obey the nudge of God. And he had a trusting heart that let God's command outweigh earthly fears.

God will give you that kind of wonderful friend from among his people. But here's a question: will you be that kind of wonderful friend for others?

READ THIS AND PRAY: A friend loves at all times, and a brother is born for adversity (Proverbs 17:17).

A man of many companions may come to ruin, but there is a friend who sticks closer than a brother (Proverbs 18:24).

Prayer: Thank you, Lord Jesus, for my Christian friends. Thank you for all the good that they have done me. Help me to be a good Christian friend too. Help me to be willing to help people when I feel your nudge in my life. Amen.

DAY 7 BIBLE READING
2 CORINTHIANS 4:6-7

⁶For God, who said, "Let light shine out of darkness," made his light shine in our hearts to give us the light of the knowledge of the glory of God in the face of Christ. ⁷But we have this treasure in jars of clay to show that this all-surpassing power is from God and not from us.

WHAT CAN YOU DO TO GET TO HEAVEN? Will going to church, reading the Bible and praying get you there? No. In fact, there is nothing you can do to win a place in heaven. Sin is too terrible and heaven is too wonderful for that. Even good people have sinned and sin deserves punishment. The good news is that Jesus loves sinners so much that he died for them. We all need to be forgiven and only Jesus can do that. When we are forgiven for our sins we are also given the gift of eternal life. Heaven will one day be the home of all those who love and trust in the Lord Jesus Christ.

DISCIPLES: Jesus chose twelve disciples to be his special companions. These disciples came to be known as the twelve apostles. However, Judas, the one who betrayed Jesus, was replaced by Matthias. The word 'disciple' also refers to people today who follow Jesus.

FEAR: "Do not be afraid" is the most common command in the Bible. It is given 366 times. Once for every day of the year – and the leap year!

THINK ABOUT IT: DAY 7
2 CORINTHIANS 4:6-7
JESUS IS LORD

Jesus can do all the things that he did for Saul for you. Today we remind ourselves that he is Lord and he is able to do what you and I can't do.

When Jesus sent out the disciples in Matthew 28:16, he spoke as the one who had all authority in heaven and on earth. He had defeated the worst things – sin, death and Satan. There was nothing that he did not have command over. So today, when he sends the weak, fearful, inexperienced and nervous disciple out on the mission there won't be anything or anyone that they face that Jesus isn't Lord over. Even death has been beaten by Jesus.

It means that the mission that he calls you to join in with is bound to succeed, so we can be hopeful! It also means that we need not be afraid but can be full of courage.

READ THIS AND PRAY: The people were amazed at his teaching, because he taught them as one who had authority, not as the teachers of the law (Mark 1:22).

But the saints of the Most High will receive the kingdom and will possess it forever—yes, for ever and ever (Daniel 7:18).

Prayer: Father God, help me to trust you. Thank you that you have all authority in heaven and on earth. You are sovereign. Thank you that you have promised to be with us to the end of the world. We can trust in you to save sinners and lead us to heaven. Amen.

Words: Father; forgiven; heaven; Satan; sovereign – see pages 109-113

PART 2

PAUL STARTS TO SERVE

When God changes our lives he doesn't take us straight to heaven. We could worship him better there and we would know him better there; we wouldn't sin any more and there's no suffering there. But there's something that can't be done in heaven that God wants done on earth: he wants people to hear about him and turn to him in repentance.

Jesus said that after he had returned to heaven his followers were to tell people all over the world about him, calling people to repent and be changed from his enemies to his friends. God's patience gives time for this to happen, and what better people to talk about the difference that Jesus makes than the people he's changed? You and me! Angels couldn't do it; we are the ones who can talk abut God's saving love shown to us in Jesus.

So God didn't take Paul to heaven right away: there was work to do down here. It's the same for you and for me.

Every day is a day for serving God. But here's an interesting thing: in the Old Testament, the scriptures that Paul knew so well, the word for service is also the word for worship. When we do God's will, taking part in God's work, we are worshipping him. We're saying that his will is best, his work is the most worthwhile, he's the best person to serve – better even than serving ourselves.

And you can start to serve God as soon as your life has been changed by him. We see that this change happened in Paul's life as we read what happened immediately after his conversion.

Before we go on you might want to read Acts 9:19-26.

PART 2
ACTS 9:19-26
PAUL STARTS TO SERVE

DAY 8 BIBLE READING
Acts 9:19-20

[19] ... and after taking some food, he regained his strength.

SAUL IN DAMASCUS AND JERUSALEM

Saul spent several days with the disciples in Damascus. [20]At once he began to preach in the synagogues that Jesus is the Son of God.

PREACH: Preaching is a special job or calling given by God. When a man of God preaches he is proclaiming the Word of God. Those who listen to the Word being preached are listening to God. A preacher is God's mouthpiece to the Church of Christ and the world.

HOW CAN I WORK FOR GOD? You may not have a lot of money now but there may be a time in the future when God blesses you with a job, a car, even a house. Be sure to use God's gift for his glory. Be hospitable and welcome people to your home. Be willing to use your car to help others who are working for God's kingdom. Do not hold onto your money selfishly as if it was all yours. Instead, be like the early Christians who were willing to sell those things that they didn't need in order to give money to God's work and to other needy Christians (Acts 4:32–35).

THINK ABOUT IT: DAY 8 ACTS 9:19-20
GOD CAN MOVE QUICKLY

Some of God's work in our lives takes years, and some of the people that we are influencing for him might take years to respond. But sometimes God moves like lightning!

Luke said that Paul began to preach 'immediately'. You might not be called to preach – although you might be; don't rule it out – but you are on a mission with God as one of his witnesses. All the training is 'on the job'. We learn the job while we do it. So who has he sent you amongst today? What could you say to them today that comes from the Bible? Is there something about how God has blessed you that could bless them now? You don't need to go to college; you don't need to become an expert first; you don't need to go somewhere else to start being a witness. The circumstances might not be easier tomorrow; the moment when someone would listen might pass. If not now, when? God can use you today.

READ THIS AND PRAY: No one can serve two masters. Either he will hate the one and love the other, or he will be devoted to the one and despise the other. You cannot serve both God and Money (Matthew 6:24).
Love the Lord your God with all your heart and with all your soul and with all your mind (Matthew 22:37).

Prayer: Lord Jesus, you have called me to serve you today. You are with me today. You are Lord over all the moments of today. Thank you that even if I'm young and haven't been a Christian for very long, you can help me to be ready to be your witness today. Amen.

Words: blessed; witness – see pages 109-113

DAY 9 BIBLE READING
ACTS 9:22

22Yet Saul grew more and more powerful and baffled the Jews living in Damascus by proving that Jesus is the Christ.

KING OF KINGS: Jesus is the King of kings because he is God's chosen and promised Saviour for the whole world. But if Jesus was the King of kings why was he mocked and whipped and killed? Is this a sign of weakness? No! It's quite the opposite. Jesus was willing to suffer and die in order to save his people from their sins. The King of kings was fully in control even up to the moment of his death. Nobody took his life away, he willingly gave it for sinners.

THINK ABOUT YOUR LIFE: Are you sure that Jesus Christ is your Saviour and King?

THINK ABOUT IT: DAY 9 ACTS 9:22
YOU CAN SPEAK ABOUT JESUS

There are three things that we always want people to understand when we talk to them about Jesus: his identity – who he is; his mission – why he came; and his call – what it means for us to follow him.

Paul realised that when people saw who Jesus really was then they would be more willing to listen to the other things about him – such as why he came and what it means to follow him. Paul wanted people to know that Jesus is the king that God had sent to be Saviour and Lord. Titles such as 'the Christ', 'the Messiah', or 'God's anointed one', mean just that – Jesus is King.

There's no real Christianity without that. Christianity is not our behaviour or our group of friends or our country's religion. It's accepting Jesus as King, the only one who saves us.

READ THIS AND PRAY: It is my pleasure to tell you about the miraculous signs and wonders that the Most High God has performed for me. How great are his signs, how mighty his wonders! His kingdom is an eternal kingdom; his dominion endures from generation to generation (Daniel 4:2-3).

Prayer: Lord Jesus, thank you for who you are. Help me to let my friends see the truth about you today. Amen.

Boot Camp: 003/Introducing Jesus – see page 118
Words: Saviour – see pages 109-113
Who's Who: Jesus – see page 114

DAY 10 BIBLE READING
Acts 9:23-26

²³After many days had gone by, the Jews conspired to kill him, ²⁴but Saul learned of their plan. Day and night they kept close watch on the city gates in order to kill him. ²⁵But his followers took him by night and lowered him in a basket through an opening in the wall.

²⁶When he came to Jerusalem, he tried to join the disciples, but they were all afraid of him, not believing that he really was a disciple.

MISSIONARY: This is someone who is committed to telling others the good news about Jesus Christ. So if you are a follower of Jesus then you too are a missionary because we should all be concerned about spreading the gospel. Sometimes missionaries go abroad to tell people from other countries about Jesus; they are called overseas missionaries. But you don't have to go to another country to work as a missionary. You can be a missionary in your own country and even in your own street.

THINK ABOUT IT: DAY 10 ACTS 9:23-26
IT'S NOT AN EASY THING TO DO

Paul very quickly discovers that being a disciple of Jesus and being a part of Jesus' mission team isn't easy. Some people listen and believe. But some people feel so threatened by the message that they become angry. They reject the message, they reject Jesus, and so they reject Paul.

Paul would have understood exactly how they felt. Remember that only a short while before, he had been doing exactly the same thing. In fact, God converted him when he was on his way to Damascus to join with these very Jews in their attempt to wipe out the name of Jesus. Now he has switched sides: the Jews see him as a traitor.

There is a special kind of anger that people have for one of their own kind. In many parts of the world today followers of Jesus face the fiercest hatred from their own families and friends. Jesus said this would happen. So if you find that some people really don't like your Christianity, don't be worried. Pray for them with love, ask Jesus to make you brave and faithful to him and get on with the rest of life without hatred in your own heart.

READ THIS AND PRAY: You have heard that it was said, 'Love your neighbour and hate your enemy.' But I tell you: Love your enemies and pray for those who persecute you, that you may be sons of your Father in heaven. He causes his sun to rise on the evil and the good, and sends rain on the righteous and the unrighteous (Matthew 5:43-45).

Prayer: Heavenly Father, help me to be faithful, true and bold. Help me also to be full of love. Take fear and hatred from my heart. Amen.

Words: disciple; believe; converted; faithful; righteous; Jews – see pages 109-113.

DAY 11 BIBLE READING
LUKE 9:57-62

THE COST OF FOLLOWING JESUS

[57]As they were walking along the road, a man said to him, "I will follow you wherever you go."

[58]Jesus replied, "Foxes have holes and birds of the air have nests, but the Son of Man has no place to lay his head."

[59]He said to another man, "Follow me." But the man replied, "Lord, first let me go and bury my father."

[60]Jesus said to him, "Let the dead bury their own dead, but you go and proclaim the kingdom of God."

[61] Still another said, "I will follow you, Lord; but first let me go back and say goodbye to my family."

[62]Jesus replied, "No one who puts his hand to the plough and looks back is fit for service in the kingdom of God."

KINGDOM: Jesus is described as the King of kings. All kings have kingdoms that they rule over. Kings have subjects in their kingdoms over whom they rule, govern and defend. How is Jesus a king? He does exactly what a king does. He rules us and defends us and he restrains and conquers our enemies – sin and the devil. God has a kingdom. He rules earth and heaven; the universe is under his command. But when we talk about God building his kingdom what we mean is that God is bringing people into his family. God's kingdom is made up of people who love and are subject to trust in him. When we build God's kingdom we are working to make sure that other people know about the good news that Jesus saves sinners.

Think about it: DAY 11 Luke 9:57-62
Jesus is with you all the time

Yesterday we mentioned that Jesus told us that his followers will be hated by some people. We asked our heavenly Father to take fear from our hearts.

God is so very good to us. Jesus promised that when people hate us because we are following him, living his way and telling the truth about him, he will help us.

In Matthew 5:11-12 he said that we should be glad and have joy because there will be a great reward in heaven for us. He also said that we should be glad that we are in good company when we suffer for his sake – God's Old Testament prophets faced the same thing. He also said that the Holy Spirit will help us to know what to say (Luke 12:12). The one who sends us into the world has overcome the world (John 16:33) and has promised that he will be with us all the time (Matthew 28:20).

So do not be afraid – you are on a mission with God!

READ THIS AND PRAY: Consider it pure joy, my brothers, whenever you face trials of many kinds, because you know that the testing of your faith develops perseverance. Perseverance must finish its work so that you may be mature and complete, not lacking anything (James 1:2-4).

Prayer: Thank you, Jesus, that you will be with me all the time today. I need not be afraid to be your follower or your fellow-missionary. Holy Spirit, help me to know what to say today if the need arises. Amen.

Words: heaven; prophet – see pages 109-113
Boot Camp 001/Getting started with you – Heaven – page 116

PART 3

THE FIRST MISSIONARY JOURNEY

Paul is on a mission: you're on it too! At the beginning of the book of Acts, Jesus says that after the Holy Spirit is sent to the Church Jesus' followers would be his witnesses in Jerusalem, Judea, Samaria and to the ends of the earth (Acts 1:8).

Jesus described two things there: his people and the places that they would go with the gospel.

His followers were to tell others what they had seen and heard when they had been with Jesus. His teaching and his commands, his miracles and the way he treated people, his death on the cross and his resurrection from the grave – all these were to become a message about King Jesus. And the message was to be proclaimed so that people who heard it would repent and turn to Jesus for eternal life.

The followers were to start to tell this message right where they were: Jerusalem. But they wouldn't stay there. The message had to go out to the countryside and the towns and villages around the capital. But it had to go further: to Samaria to the north where many people with a Jewish background lived. And then it had to go away out to the rest of the world: to Europe, Africa, Asia, India, the Americas – to all nations and languages.

God's mission is for all Jesus' followers in the whole world. That means you and me, wherever God puts us. God is on his mission.

Paul was now on God's mission and you and I are on it too!

Over the next eight days we'll follow Paul and his great friend, Barnabas, on the first missionary journey that they made, taking the gospel into places where it had never been heard before, to people who had never heard of Jesus. The route that they took is on the map. (See page 126 – First Missionary Journey.)

You and I might not be sent by our churches to go to other countries. You might be when you're older so keep listening to see where God wants you to be. But God has put us where we are now so that we can tell the good news about King Jesus. What we read over the next eight days has plenty to teach us even if we never go anywhere else in life other than where we're living right now. God is sending you into the world today as one of his missionaries because that's what every Christian is: a missionary.

PART 3

ACTS 13&14

THE FIRST JOURNEY: PAUL IS ON A MISSION –
YOU'RE ON IT TOO!

DAY 12 BIBLE READING
MATTHEW 28:16-20

THE GREAT COMMISSION

[16]Then the eleven disciples went to Galilee, to the mountain where Jesus had told them to go. [17]When they saw him, they worshipped him; but some doubted. [18]Then Jesus came to them and said, "All authority in heaven and on earth has been given to me. [19]Therefore go and make disciples of all nations, baptizing them in the name of the Father and of the Son and of the Holy Spirit, [20]and teaching them to obey everything I have commanded you. And surely I am with you always, to the very end of the age."

GOSPEL: This word means good news. Think about the different kinds of good news you can get. God's good news is much better. God's good news for us is that our sins can be forgiven and that he loves us. Through Christ's death we can be saved from the punishment of sin. God sets his people free and God keeps them safe – forever.

THINK ABOUT IT: DAY 12
MATTHEW 28:16-20
YOUR MISSION: CHANGE THE WORLD ...

But one step at a time!

Near the end of the Bible, in Revelation 11:15, we read of voices in heaven saying loudly, 'The kingdom of this world has become the kingdom of our God and of his Christ, and he will reign for ever and ever'. Just as God used Paul so he also will use all his followers to do nothing less than change the world.

Paul's special mission was to take the gospel to those who weren't Jews; but he had to start with the Jews. Along with Barnabas he taught new converts in the great city of Antioch. The church in Antioch decided to send Paul, Barnabas and others on a journey with the gospel to plant new churches, mostly in areas where many Jews as well as non-Jews (Gentiles) lived.

So the gospel came to your country because nearly two thousand years ago Paul and Barnabas took a step with the gospel – then another, and another and another and ...

READ THIS AND PRAY: In the same way, let your light shine before men, that they may see your good deeds and praise your Father in heaven (Matthew 5:16).

Prayer: Thank you, Lord, for giving me a mission in life – your mission. Thank you that my life has a purpose because of you. Thank you that I don't need to drift aimlessly through life not knowing why I'm here. I'm here to share in your work: to change the world. Amen.

Words: forgiven; gentiles; gospel; Jews; kingdom – see pages 109-113

Maps: Antioch; Galilee – see pages 126-127

DAY 13 BIBLE READING
ACTS 13:1-3

BARNABAS AND SAUL SENT OFF

¹In the church at Antioch there were prophets and teachers: Barnabas, Simeon called Niger, Lucius of Cyrene, Manaen (who had been brought up with Herod the tetrarch) and Saul. ²While they were worshipping the Lord and fasting, the Holy Spirit said, "Set apart for me Barnabas and Saul for the work to which I have called them." ³So after they had fasted and prayed, they placed their hands on them and sent them off.

THINK ABOUT YOUR LIFE: You need the people in your church. Are there older Christians that you respect? Talk to them about how you are getting on following Jesus. Ask them to pray for you. People in your church also need you. Who can you pray for? Is there a younger person in the church that you can befriend?

THINK ABOUT IT: DAY 13 ACTS 13:1-3
THE SPIRIT AND THE CHURCH

It's important to notice that Paul and his friend, Barnabas, didn't come up with the idea of going out with the gospel all on their own. They were sent by the Spirit and the church.

We're not called to be heroic individuals who don't need other people. We're part of Jesus' body, the Church. Your brothers and sisters in Jesus have been given a responsibility for you and you for them. We are all one body – you and I are just different parts of it. We will never become mature missionaries without the rest of the Church.

That's good, but not always the way we want it. It's good because other people can sometimes see us better than we see ourselves; and other people will show deeper loving support if we're in the work of God's mission together with them. It's not always what we want though because sometimes we think that other Christians – especially older ones – don't really understand us. Listening to others out of respect can really test our love!

READ THIS AND PRAY: I tell you the truth, no servant is greater than his master, nor is a messenger greater than the one who sent him (John 13:16).

Prayer: Father God, give me a willing heart to love and obey you. Guide me through your Word and show me what I ought to do. Help me to be respectful to other Christians and a servant of you, my master, willing to work hard to build up your Church. Amen.

Words: the Church (see also page 18); fasting – see pages 109-113

DAY 14 BIBLE READING
LUKE 14:27-33

27And anyone who does not carry his cross and follow me cannot be my disciple.

28Suppose one of you wants to build a tower. Will he not first sit down and estimate the cost to see if he has enough money to complete it? 29For if he lays the foundation and is not able to finish it, everyone who sees it will ridicule him, 30saying, 'This fellow began to build and was not able to finish.'

31Or suppose a king is about to go to war against another king. Will he not first sit down and consider whether he is able with ten thousand men to oppose the one coming against him with twenty thousand? 32If he is not able, he will send a delegation while the other is still a long way off and will ask for terms of peace. 33In the same way, any of you who does not give up everything he has cannot be my disciple.

THE CROSS: Crucifixion on a cross was a method of execution in Roman times – two pieces of wood to which victims were nailed, lifted up and left to die. But Jesus wasn't a victim. His death was part of God's plan. Jesus was obedient to his Father and willing to die in the place of his people. It is through him that we can have eternal life. But what now? We are told to live a life of sacrifice and to follow Jesus. The Bible tells us to lift up our cross and follow Jesus. We are to become more like him day by day.

FAITH IN JESUS: The Bible says "Faith is being sure of what we hope for and certain of what we do not see" (Hebrews 11:1). If you believe in Jesus you have a sure and certain hope that you are saved from your sin. This hope is sure and certain. A Christian's hope of heaven is a fact because Jesus has done everything necessary to make it true.

THINK ABOUT IT: DAY 14 LUKE 14:27-33
COSTLY OBEDIENCE

What do you want your future to be like? Perhaps the costliest part of being on God's mission is that we go where he says, do what pleases him. It only seems like a cost. Actually it's a great gain and it's an eternal gain. But for many of us the really hard part, and the bit that our non-Christian friends will think is really bad, is that we have to let go of our control over our future.

That control is only an illusion: we only think that we control our future. In fact we never really know what's going to happen next. Yet it's a deep rooted and precious illusion. It can be the hardest thing on earth to let go of. Even when we are learning to trust and obey God totally we still may struggle in giving up control.

As Paul and Barnabas set off they had a strategy and a route in mind. But they didn't know how things would turn out: we plan, but only God knows the outcome. Walking by faith in God costs us our sense of control over life but really it's the only sensible way to live.

READ THIS AND PRAY: And we know that in all things God works for the good of those who love him, who have been called according to his purpose (Romans 8:28).

Trust in the LORD with all your heart and lean not on your own understanding; in all your ways acknowledge him, and he will make your paths straight (Proverbs 3:5-6).

Prayer: Lord, help me to trust you for today and all my tomorrows. I have my hopes, my plans and my dreams. But help me to trust you for the way that things will work out for me on your mission. Thank you that you always make everything work out best. Amen.

Words: eternal; faith – see pages 109-113

DAY 15 BIBLE READING
ACTS 13:8-12

8But Elymas the sorcerer (for that is what his name means) opposed them and tried to turn the proconsul from the faith. 9Then Saul, who was also called Paul, filled with the Holy Spirit, looked straight at Elymas and said, 10"You are a child of the devil and an enemy of everything that is right! You are full of all kinds of deceit and trickery. Will you never stop perverting the right ways of the Lord? 11Now the hand of the Lord is against you. You are going to be blind, and for a time you will be unable to see the light of the sun."

Immediately mist and darkness came over him, and he groped about, seeking someone to lead him by the hand. 12When the proconsul saw what had happened, he believed, for he was amazed at the teaching about the Lord.

SATAN: He is God's enemy, also known as the tempter. He was the one who persuaded Adam and Eve to disobey God in the Garden of Eden, but you can read in Genesis chapter 3 about God promised to send one who would defeat Satan. That person was Jesus Christ and he defeated Satan and the power of sin and death by his death on the cross and his resurrection.

Words: Confess – see pages 109-113

Think about it: DAY 15 Acts 13:8-12
Paphos: Satan's mad at Jesus!

We are all in a spiritual battle. Satan doesn't give up easily even though Christ disarmed him on the cross.

So when the gospel came to the highly cultural and wealthy capital of Cyprus, and people started believing in Jesus, Satan tried to stop it through Elymas the sorcerer.

Paul and the others didn't back down. They knew that the person with all authority in heaven and on earth was with them, so they boldly went on the counter-attack as the Spirit filled them afresh for the fight.

And what happened? In the very moment of fierce opposition, God turned the situation right round as the Proconsul, the most important man on Cyprus, saw God's power and victory over Elymas. He believed the gospel. Satan scored an own goal!

God's enemy doesn't want you to share the good news about Jesus. When things seem to be opposing you, ask God to give you his Spirit in order to put courage in your heart, then press on to share the good news.

READ THIS AND PRAY: I press on toward the goal to win the prize for which God has called me heavenward in Christ Jesus (Philippians 3:14).

But you, man of God, flee from all this, and pursue righteousness, godliness, faith, love, endurance and gentleness. Fight the good fight of the faith. Take hold of the eternal life to which you were called when you made your good confession in the presence of many witnesses (1 Timothy 6:11-12).

Prayer: Lord, there are people around me who need the good news about Jesus. Send your Spirit afresh to me today so that I might not be a coward and shrink back, but be brave and press forwards with the gospel. Amen.

Boot Camp 003/Introducing Jesus – authority – see page 118

DAY 16 BIBLE READING
ACTS 13:47-49

⁴⁷For this is what the Lord has commanded us:

"'I have made you a light for the Gentiles, that you may bring salvation to the ends of the earth.'"

⁴⁸When the Gentiles heard this, they were glad and honoured the word of the Lord; and all who were appointed for eternal life believed.

⁴⁹The word of the Lord spread through the whole region.

GENTILES: This is the word used to describe people who aren't Jewish. The gospel of Jesus Christ came to the Jewish people first, but then to the Gentiles. It was always part of God's plan that the good news of salvation would come to the whole world (Matthew 4:12-17).

THINK ABOUT IT: DAY 16 ACTS 13:47-49 PISIDIAN ANTIOCH: LOVE GOD AND BE FLEXIBLE

We have our ideas; God has his! Paul and Barnabas arrived in a lovely multicultural city on a high plateau dotted with lakes. They started to teach the gospel to the Jews there. They were doing what God called them to do and they were doing it bravely and brilliantly well.

But the Jews would have nothing of it. Luke then recorded some of the most significant words in the history of God's mission: 'we now turn to the Gentiles' (verse 46). The whole course of the Church and the world changed at that point. Those words were like a hinge that God's mission turned on that day. The good news about Jesus was for the Gentiles, for all the world: the one who was crucified as 'King of the Jews' was dying for the sins of people everywhere. His kingdom would be made up of people from every tribe and language, people and nation (Revelation 5:9).

What if Paul and Barnabas had been too stuck in their own ideas of how things would go? You see, God wants you to be flexible enough to change your own plans to suit his.

READ THIS AND PRAY: Observe the commands of the LORD your God, walking in his ways and revering him (Deuteronomy 8:6).

I obey your precepts and your statutes, for all my ways are known to you (Psalm 119:168).

Prayer: Father, your ways are not my ways and your thoughts are not my thoughts. Please help me not to get stuck in my ways or too fixed on my ideas. Help me to follow you, wherever you want me to go to, on your mission. Amen.

Words: crucified; salvation – see pages 109-113

DAY 17 BIBLE READING
ACTS 14:1-7

IN ICONIUM

[1]At Iconium Paul and Barnabas went as usual into the Jewish synagogue. There they spoke so effectively that a great number of Jews and Gentiles believed. [2]But the Jews who refused to believe stirred up the Gentiles and poisoned their minds against the brothers. [3]So Paul and Barnabas spent considerable time there, speaking boldly for the Lord, who confirmed the message of his grace by enabling them to do miraculous signs and wonders. [4]The people of the city were divided; some sided with the Jews, others with the apostles. [5]There was a plot afoot among the Gentiles and Jews, together with their leaders, to mistreat them and stone them. [6]But they found out about it and fled to the Lycaonian cities of Lystra and Derbe and to the surrounding country, [7]where they continued to preach the good news.

THINK ABOUT YOUR LIFE: Your mind matters to God. Write down some of the reasons why it matters so much to him. As you go through the day, make a mental note of the ways in which your non-Christian friends think about God, about life and about you. What does the Bible have to say about some of their ideas?

THINK ABOUT IT: DAY 17 ACTS 14:1-7
ICONIUM: THERE'S A BATTLE FOR YOUR
MIND

The Jews wanted to stop the mission to the Gentiles in Iconium. So they 'poisoned' the minds of the Gentiles against those who preached the truth of Jesus Christ.

God's enemy, Satan, can do the same to the minds of your friends and family who do not trust in Jesus. He can poison their minds against the gospel. The devil's evil schemes can make your work much more difficult.

Some people think that they are being very clever to say that there is no God or that it doesn't matter what you believe. Many of your friends will be already convinced that you can drink as much as you want, have sex with whoever you want to, use drugs however you want and live for money and self. Their minds are already poisoned against the gospel of Jesus.

So you need to be ready with answers. Which is why reading your Bible will help you so much, and why listening to the Bible being taught in church will equip you for the fight. You need to be brave enough not to back down. You need to be careful about your own mind too.

READ THIS AND PRAY: Do not conform any longer to the pattern of this world, but be transformed by the renewing of your mind. Then you will be able to test and approve what God's will is—his good, pleasing and perfect will (Romans 12:2).

Finally, brothers, whatever is true, whatever is noble, whatever is right, whatever is pure, whatever is lovely, whatever is admirable— if anything is excellent or praiseworthy—think about such things (Philippians 4:8).

Prayer: Dear Lord, help me to be able to focus my mind on your gospel, on the pure and good things that you want my mind to think about. Help me to be able to reach out to friends and family with this wonderful truth. Amen.

DAY 18 BIBLE READING
Acts 14:8-15

IN LYSTRA AND DERBE

⁸In Lystra there sat a man crippled in his feet, who was lame from birth and had never walked. ⁹He listened to Paul as he was speaking. Paul looked directly at him, saw that he had faith to be healed ¹⁰and called out, "Stand up on your feet!" At that, the man jumped up and began to walk.

¹¹When the crowd saw what Paul had done, they shouted in the Lycaonian language, "The gods have come down to us in human form!" ¹²Barnabas they called Zeus, and Paul they called Hermes because he was the chief speaker. ¹³The priest of Zeus, whose temple was just outside the city, brought bulls and wreaths to the city gates because he and the crowd wanted to offer sacrifices to them.

¹⁴But when the apostles Barnabas and Paul heard of this, they tore their clothes and rushed out into the crowd, shouting: ¹⁵"Men, why are you doing this? We too are only men, human like you. We are bringing you good news, telling you to turn from these worthless things to the living God, who made heaven and earth and sea and everything in them.

HUMILITY: Do you ever boss or lord it over people who are younger or less able than you? That is not the way that Jesus behaves and it is not the way that his followers should behave. Jesus tells us that his followers are to be like servants. They are to be humble. They are to be more concerned about others than about themselves. Jesus was exactly like this.

THINK ABOUT IT: DAY 18 ACTS 14:8-15
LYSTRA AND DERBE: YOU'RE NOT GOD!

It might seem like a little point in the passage, but it's really important that, like Paul and Barnabas, we don't take God's place. If we start thinking that we are better than other people we will lose our love for God, our love for others and our desire to tell others about him. We'll turn God's mission into ours. We'll seek glory for ourselves and not for God. We'll start taking credit that should be given to other people. And it will become obvious to everyone that we've become hard-hearted.

Why? Well, when Paul and Barnabas said 'We too are only men, human like you' they were making several things clear. Firstly: only the one true God is to be worshipped – the false gods of Lystra aren't to be worshipped. Secondly: the messengers are only messengers – the important thing about them is the message that they carry. And finally: the messengers needed the same work of grace through Jesus that everyone else needs. What Paul and Barnabas said pointed people away from error to the truth; away from themselves to God; away from sinful pride to humble trust and obedience.

READ THIS AND PRAY: Humble yourselves before the Lord, and he will lift you up (James 4:10).
He has showed you, O man, what is good. And what does the LORD require of you? To act justly and to love mercy and to walk humbly with your God (Micah 6:8).

Prayer: Lord, don't let me get above myself. Let me be full of you and your love and glory – not full of myself. Help me to point people to you alone. Amen.

Words: worship; grace; temple – see pages 109-113

DAY 19 BIBLE READING
ACTS 14:21-23

THE RETURN TO ANTIOCH IN SYRIA

[21]They preached the good news in that city and won a large number of disciples. Then they returned to Lystra, Iconium and Antioch, [22]strengthening the disciples and encouraging them to remain true to the faith. "We must go through many hardships to enter the kingdom of God," they said. [23]Paul and Barnabas appointed elders for them in each church and, with prayer and fasting, committed them to the Lord, in whom they had put their trust.

FAITH: It is amazing what faith in God achieves. It is not because our faith is amazing that it accomplishes anything – it is because of the God in whom we have our faith. (See also Words on pages 109-113.)

Think about it: DAY 19 Acts 14:21-23
God's Training Course for you

Paul and Barnabas didn't end their mission when they got back to Antioch. Everything that God had shown them on the first journey was a preparation for the next one, part of a lifelong training course. The future that lay before them was changing because God was – and still is – at work. He is constantly creative, the kingdom is constantly growing, and people are constantly changing. New opportunities open up for the gospel, new temptations come our way, we ourselves change. There is always more to learn; God is always training us – preparing us – for the next step.

Much of that preparation comes in the difficult time. We tend to learn less and depend on God less when things are going well for us. We can be tempted to start trusting ourselves so that pride takes root in our hearts. As Paul said to Jesus' followers, 'We must go through many hardships to enter the kingdom of God.'

So if you have been seeking to be a good missionary but you feel like a failure in your attempts to follow God in his mission, don't be discouraged. God will use those difficulties to build your faith in him. Everything from today will help you walk with the Lord tomorrow.

READ THIS AND PRAY: It is better to take refuge in the LORD than to trust in man. It is better to take refuge in the LORD than to trust in princes (Psalm 119:8-9).
You will keep in perfect peace him whose mind is steadfast, because he trusts in you (Isaiah 26:3).

Prayer: Thank you, Lord, that you will always teach me new ways to serve you. Keep me ready to learn, and help me to trust your wisdom as you train me throughout my life. Amen.

Words: temptation; pride – see pages 109-113.

PART 4

PAUL IS ONLY HUMAN: SO ARE YOU!

One of the things about not being in heaven yet is that we live with the effects of sin in the world and in our own hearts. We've all got problems and we all struggle with weakness, temptation and inner problems. Maybe you've got a temper that can flare up in a moment. Maybe you feel that everyone's against you and you often feel sorry for yourself. Maybe things that people have said or done have left you very deeply hurt and it comes out as anger. Perhaps you always see the best in people and can't see their weaknesses; or perhaps you don't trust anyone and can't see their potential.

Paul and his great friend, Barnabas, were human just like you and me. Paul wasn't perfect and he was ready to admit it. Over the next four days we look at the big fall-out between Paul and Barnabas. But we're going to see what happened that day in Antioch against the background of God's long-term work in their lives. What gets spoiled here on earth will be put right in heaven. Sometimes it seems like the devil has won a victory in our lives; but God will always turn it around so that his purposes for us win through in the end. God's mission carried on, and it still continues. At the end of your life, the score line will be God 1 – Satan 0. God never loses; he always wins even if the final whistle seems a long way off.

It's good that we have the story of Paul and Barnabas falling out. The Bible is very honest about God's missionaries. None of Jesus' followers is perfect so don't think that others are, and don't be down-hearted when you realise that you're not. If you know your weaknesses you're stronger for it, and you're in very good company!

The story is in Acts 15:36-41.

Part 4
Acts 15:36-41
Paul is only Human: so are you!

DAY 20 BIBLE READING
ACTS 15:36–41

36Some time later Paul said to Barnabas, "Let us go back and visit the brothers in all the towns where we preached the Word of the Lord and see how they are doing." 37Barnabas wanted to take John, also called Mark, with them, 38but Paul did not think it wise to take him, because he had deserted them in Pamphylia and had not continued with them in the work. 39They had such a sharp disagreement that they parted company. Barnabas took Mark and sailed for Cyprus, 40but Paul chose Silas and left, commended by the brothers to the grace of the Lord. 41He went through Syria and Cilicia, strengthening the churches.

THINK ABOUT IT: DAY 20 ACTS 15:36-41
PAUL AND BARNABAS FALL-OUT

These two men had strong views but very different approaches to people. And as a result they had a really stormy row over John Mark. Was he suitable to take with them on the second journey? Would he be reliable or would he cut and run like he had last time, when they were in Pamphylia (Acts 15:38)? John Mark can't have been all that bad since Paul asked for him to be sent to him later in his life; and he did write the second of our four Gospels. But whatever the rights and wrongs concerning him going on their second voyage the two men shouldn't have split up the way they did.

Well, that's easy for us to say, isn't it? But haven't you ever had a huge row with a good friend? Don't you always want to win an argument? Haven't we all got so boiled up over something that we've lost sight of the Lord's love?

So it's strangely encouraging to read that two of the greatest missionaries who have ever lived were human just like you and me. Jesus knows that we all have a button which, if pushed even by a friend, will make us explode with anger and not back down. God doesn't expect you to be perfect; he does want you to be willing.

READ THIS AND PRAY: Each of you must put off falsehood and speak truthfully to his neighbour, for we are all members of one body. "In your anger do not sin": Do not let the sun go down while you are still angry, and do not give the devil a foothold (Ephesians 4:25-27).

Turn from evil and do good; seek peace and pursue it (Psalm 34:14).

Prayer: Lord, I come to you as a weak human being with many faults. It is amazing that you have chosen someone like me to glorify your perfect Son today. I praise your holy name, and ask you to forgive me when I have been angry and fallen out with a friend. Help me to make it up with them. Amen.

Maps: Cyprus; Pamphylia; Syria; Cilicia – see pages 126-127

DAY 21 BIBLE READING2
Timothy 2:22-26

²²Flee the evil desires of youth, and pursue righteousness, faith, love and peace, along with those who call on the Lord out of a pure heart. ²³Don't have anything to do with foolish and stupid arguments, because you know they produce quarrels. ²⁴And the Lord's servant must not quarrel; instead, he must be kind to everyone, able to teach, not resentful. ²⁵Those who oppose him he must gently instruct, in the hope that God will grant them repentance leading them to a knowledge of the truth, ²⁶and that they will come to their senses and escape from the trap of the devil, who has taken them captive to do his will.

THINK ABOUT IT: DAY 21
2 TIMOTHY 2:22-26 BE WISE

There are three other lessons to draw out from this incident. The first is *be wise*.

After great blessing often comes great failure. Elijah was on the mountain-top one day and in the depths of despair the next day (1 Kings 18–19). David was doing brilliantly as a king one day and by the next morning he had committed adultery (2 Samuel 10–11). Abraham was given massively wonderful promises from God about his offspring and then he shows the most ridiculous fear of Pharaoh (Genesis 12).

You see, the devil knows that we are usually off-guard when things are going well. He can sneak up to us with a temptation and in an instant make the most of our weaknesses. Maybe we think too highly of ourselves; maybe we're too convinced by other people's praise and we forget to give glory to the God who has saved us; maybe we're just tired. Satan will lunge at us when things are going well; he hates it when God is glorified through our weak lives. So be wise and when you are seeing blessing in your mission with God, watch out!

READ THIS AND PRAY: Be self-controlled and alert. Your enemy the devil prowls around like a roaring lion looking for someone to devour. Resist him, standing firm in the faith, because you know that your brothers throughout the world are undergoing the same kind of sufferings (1 Peter 5:8-9).

Prayer: Lord, help me to remember that the devil prowls around looking for someone to devour. Keep me as watchful as if I lived among wild wolves. Amen.

Words: devil; repentance; temptation – see pages 109-113

Who's Who: Abraham; David; Elijah – see page 114

DAY 22 BIBLE READING
ROMANS 7:21-25

²¹So I find this law at work: When I want to do good, evil is right there with me. ²²For in my inner being I delight in God's law; ²³but I see another law at work in the members of my body, waging war against the law of my mind and making me a prisoner of the law of sin at work within my members. ²⁴What a wretched man I am! Who will rescue me from this body of death? ²⁵Thanks be to God—through Jesus Christ our Lord!

So then, I myself in my mind am a slave to God's law, but in the sinful nature a slave to the law of sin.

THINK ABOUT YOUR LIFE: Who do you need to forgive? Perhaps someone has disappointed you. Perhaps someone simply hasn't lived up to your expectations. Were your expectations reasonable or are your standards high for others and not so high for yourself?

THINK ABOUT IT: DAY 22
ROMANS 7:21-25 BE REALISTIC

Every Christian you've ever met – even the ones you admire the most – is a sinner just like you.

The people that you respect the most, or envy for their Bible knowledge or their gifts or popularity, are clothed in frail flesh like you. They can be led astray by the tempter; drink, power, pornography, bitterness, greed, dishonesty, pride – all this and more can lurk in any Christian's heart. We're not in heaven yet!

Later in his life, imprisoned and writing to one of the churches planted on the second journey, Paul would write, 'I am confident of this, that he who began a good work in you will carry it on to completion until the day of Christ' (Philippians 1:6). Paul had no confidence in his own ability to make them just like Jesus; he had no confidence in their abiliity either! All his confidence was in God, who would take the rest of their lives over this important work, but who alone would make them perfect.

So *be realistic* and don't expect too much from your brothers and sisters in the Lord Jesus.

READ THIS AND PRAY: But blessed is the man who trusts in the LORD, whose confidence is in him (Jeremiah 17:7). Such confidence as this is ours through Christ before God. Not that we are competent in ourselves to claim anything for ourselves, but our competence comes from God (2 Corinthians 3:4-5).

Prayer: Lord God, help me to have confidence in you. You are going to complete the good work in me. You have said so. Help me to trust in you and be patient with others who are sinners in need of a Saviour, as I am. Amen.

Words: envy; sinner – see pages 109-113

DAY 23 BIBLE READING
REVELATION 21:1-5

THE NEW JERUSALEM

¹Then I saw a new heaven and a new earth, for the first heaven and the first earth had passed away, and there was no longer any sea. ²I saw the Holy City, the new Jerusalem, coming down out of heaven from God, prepared as a bride beautifully dressed for her husband. ³And I heard a loud voice from the throne saying, "Now the dwelling of God is with men, and he will live with them. They will be his people, and God himself will be with them and be their God. ⁴He will wipe every tear from their eyes. There will be no more death or mourning or crying or pain, for the old order of things has passed away."

⁵He who was seated on the throne said, "I am making everything new!" Then he said, "Write this down, for these words are trustworthy and true."

ADAM'S FIRST SIN: The aftershocks of Adam's first sin are all other sin and its consequences. Adam and Eve are the only human beings who knew what it was like to be without sin. Their family were born in sin and every child since then has been a sinner. We are all born with a sinful nature. All this sin and misery is the result of Adam's first sin. The consequences of that first sin include sickness, disease and death. The sweat and toil that we have to go through in order to survive is a result of sin. The pain that women go through in childbirth is a consequence of sin. But just as sin came into the world through one man so salvation comes into the world through one – Jesus Christ – who is both God and man. That is why Jesus is sometimes called the Second Adam.

THINK ABOUT IT: DAY 23
REVELATION 21:1-5 BE PATIENT

The day will come when God will put right all that sin has messed up. Paul and Barnabas fell out all those years ago; but the day will come when Jesus returns and Paul and Barnabas will be with him, together again, forever. And they'll never argue again!

However messy life gets on earth, the day will come – the great and glorious day when Christ appears, when all the aftershocks of Adam's first sin are ended. Death will die and Satan will be thrown into the fiery lake (another word for Hell). Then he will never torment God's people again. Christ's followers shall rise and see Jesus and be made like him. The day is coming when there will be no more sorrow or crying or pain, no more death, no more tears, no more sin.

So *be patient*. God's mission – which embraces all believers – will reach its fulfilment; it will succeed. Let the failings of friends, as well as your own, make you look all the more longingly for Jesus to return.

READ THIS AND PRAY: For the Lamb at the centre of the throne will be their shepherd; he will lead them to springs of living water. And God will wipe away every tear from their eyes (Revelation 7:17).

He will wipe every tear from their eyes. There will be no more death or mourning or crying or pain, for the old order of things has passed away (Revelation 21:4).

Prayer: Thank you, Father, that Jesus will return and put everything right again. Help me to wait patiently even though I long for that day to come. Help me to be patient with people, knowing that you have not finished your work in them yet. Amen.

Boot Camp 001/Getting Started with you – Punishment; Hell – see page 116
Boot Camp 004/In the Beginning – The Fall – see page 120

PART 5

PAUL'S SECOND MISSIONARY JOURNEY – YOUR HEART AND GOD'S MISSION

At some point in our lives we discover what we've got a real passion for. There will be something that really fires us up. There may even be several things that we get excited about. We find time and energy for these things, they put a smile on our face and present us with challenges that we love to rise to.

Some of these things can dominate the whole of our lives. I know someone who collects buttons. Wherever she is in the world she will keep her eyes open for interesting buttons to add to her vast collection. Another friend is mad keen on rally driving; he will travel miles to stand outside all day in freezing temperatures in a forest to be a marshal at a rally. He'd never do that for anything else – except, perhaps, for his wife!

What's going to be the all-consuming passion of your life? For many of your friends it might be money, or fashion; it might be drugs or sex; it might be sport or it might be work. For Paul, the all-consuming passion of his life became God's mission.

That's not such a weird thing if you think about it for a moment. In fact it's a brilliant way to live. If the thing you want to be doing most in life is also the thing that God wants you to be doing most in life, then even when it's tough you are on the winning side.

Over the next six days we follow Paul on his second missionary journey. Like the first journey, it's a thriller with twists and turns and surprises that we'd never have been able to predict. But on this journey Paul's heart became fixed on the thing that he would spend his life on: God's mission.

So what about the all-consuming passion in your life?

To get the big picture of Paul's second journey look at the map on page 126 and read Acts 15:40–18:22.

Part 5
Acts 15:40 – 18:2
Paul's Second Missionary Journey:
Your Heart and God's Mission

DAY 24 BIBLE READING
Acts 16:25-34

²⁵About midnight Paul and Silas were praying and singing hymns to God, and the other prisoners were listening to them. ²⁶Suddenly there was such a violent earthquake that the foundations of the prison were shaken. At once all the prison doors flew open, and everybody's chains came loose. ²⁷The jailer woke up, and when he saw the prison doors open, he drew his sword and was about to kill himself because he thought the prisoners had escaped. ²⁸But Paul shouted, "Don't harm yourself! We are all here!"

²⁹The jailer called for lights, rushed in and fell trembling before Paul and Silas. ³⁰He then brought them out and asked, "Sirs, what must I do to be saved?"

³¹They replied, "Believe in the Lord Jesus, and you will be saved— you and your household." ³²Then they spoke the word of the Lord to him and to all the others in his house. ³³At that hour of the night the jailer took them and washed their wounds; then immediately he and all his family were baptized. ³⁴The jailer brought them into his house and set a meal before them; he was filled with joy because he had come to believe in God—he and his whole family.

PRAISE: One of the ways that the Bible describes praising God is making a joyful noise to the Lord. Look up the following Bible verses to find out the different places this expression is used: Psalm 66:1; Psalm 81:1; Psalm 95:1-2; Psalm 98:4&6; Psalm 100:1.

Maps: Philippi – see pages 126-127

Words: persecution (See fact file on page 72); repent; testimony – see pages 109-113

THINK ABOUT IT: DAY 24 ACTS 16:25-34
PHILIPPI: PRAISING GOD IN PRISON

What a great time in Philippi! God got them there through a dream. They shared the good news about Jesus with some women and the Lord opened the heart of one of them and opened Europe to the gospel. The history of the Church in Europe can be traced back to that amazing Saturday morning.

Persecution followed however. Some people in the city were enraged by the missionaries so they had Paul and Silas tried, stripped, beaten and thrown into prison. But before God rescued them with an earthquake (handy!) look at what they were doing while they were chained up. They were praising God with songs! Not moaning; not grumbling at God; not wavering in their faith; not feeling sorry for themselves. No, they were singing praise to God. I bet God was pleased with that! What a testimony to the other inmates and that Philippian jailer who was to repent after the earthquake.

Are you quick to moan? Learn to sing God's praise!

READ THIS AND PRAY: Though you have not seen him, you love him; and even though you do not see him now, you believe in him and are filled with an inexpressible and glorious joy, for you are receiving the goal of your faith, the salvation of your souls (1 Peter 1:8-9).

PRAYER: Lord, give me a heart and a mouth that are quick to feel glad about you and just as quick to sing your praises. Give me the faith and thankful joy that cannot be kept in, that have to come out in songs of praise and worship. Amen.

DAY 25 BIBLE READING

ACTS 17:2-5

[2]As his custom was, Paul went into the synagogue, and on three Sabbath days he reasoned with them from the Scriptures, [3]explaining and proving that the Christ had to suffer and rise from the dead. "This Jesus I am proclaiming to you is the Christ," he said. [4]Some of the Jews were persuaded and joined Paul and Silas, as did a large number of God-fearing Greeks and not a few prominent women.

[5]But the Jews were jealous; so they rounded up some bad characters from the marketplace, formed a mob and started a riot in the city. They rushed to Jason's house in search of Paul and Silas in order to bring them out to the crowd.

PERSECUTION: Jesus has told us that, because he was hated by people, those who followed him would also be hated. So persecution is something that we should expect. Persecution is being unfairly and cruelly treated because of what we believe. People will try and make things difficult for Christians. Jesus said, in Matthew chapter 5, that those who are persecuted are blessed, for the kingdom of heaven belongs to them. Jesus has told us that when we are treated wrongly and have to suffer for loving Jesus we can rejoice because there will be a great reward for us in heaven.

Maps: Macedonia – see page 126

THINK ABOUT IT: DAY 25 ACTS 17:2-5
THESSALONICA: FACING JEALOUSY AND
MOVING ON

The response to the preaching of the gospel in the capital of ancient Macedonia was terrific. Amazingly quickly a church grew and withstood fierce opposition and persecution.

Some of that persecution came because of simple jealousy. When God draws people to Jesus, their families or their boyfriends or girlfriends might be jealous that someone new seems to be on the scene. Now the Christian no longer follows the old paths or the old crowd. Anticipate this. Don't let it put you off your work as a missionary when jealousy and hostility are aimed at you. You may be used by the Father to lead these people to Jesus.

When the jealousy turned into a riot Paul and Silas had to leave. And they could! You see, they had every confidence in God to look after the new believers. They had the gospel that Paul had taught and they had the Holy Spirit in their hearts. Paul knew that the future of the kingdom didn't rest on his shoulders, but on Jesus' shoulders. It still does; so we can leave if we need to. We can trust Jesus to do the job.

READ THIS AND PRAY: Blessed are you when people insult you, persecute you and falsely say all kinds of evil against you because of me. Rejoice and be glad, because great is your reward in heaven, for in the same way they persecuted the prophets who were before you (Matthew 5:11-12). We are hard pressed on every side, but not crushed; perplexed, but not in despair; persecuted, but not abandoned; struck down, but not destroyed (2 Corinthians 4:8-9).

Prayer: Lord, I bring to you those who have become Christians and now suffer persecution from their family, friends, colleagues or neighbours. Help them to keep trusting you and not to become bitter. And please show the jealous ones that they also need Jesus. Amen.

DAY 26 BIBLE READING
Acts 17:10-15

IN BEREA

[10]As soon as it was night, the brothers sent Paul and Silas away to Berea. On arriving there, they went to the Jewish synagogue. [11]Now the Bereans were of more noble character than the Thessalonians, for they received the message with great eagerness and examined the Scriptures every day to see if what Paul said was true. [12]Many of the Jews believed, as did also a number of prominent Greek women and many Greek men.

[13]When the Jews in Thessalonica learned that Paul was preaching the word of God at Berea, they went there too, agitating the crowds and stirring them up. [14]The brothers immediately sent Paul to the coast, but Silas and Timothy stayed at Berea. [15]The men who escorted Paul brought him to Athens and then left with instructions for Silas and Timothy to join him as soon as possible.

THINK ABOUT IT: DAY 26 ACTS 17:10-15
BEREA: HOW TO LISTEN TO SERMONS

In the next city down the coast, Berea, Paul met some really good people who knew how to listen to sermons.

Some sermons are really boring and they seem very long.

Some are very entertaining with lots of jokes and stories; those preachers can be very popular.

Some sermons sound very powerful and maybe a bit bossy; sometimes a preacher can sound very clever but he might be making it up.

Well, the Bereans knew how to listen. They were eager for God's Word, and they tested what Paul and Silas said to see if it matched what God had said in his Word. They weren't cynical but they weren't stupid and unthoughtful either. They didn't assume that everything Paul or Silas said was really from God – so they checked it out from the Bible. They were eager for God's Word, not Paul's words.

So don't be taken in by people who just sound good – check what you hear against what the Bible says. A good preacher will always help you do that by preaching from a passage that you can read for yourself. So that you can examine the Scriptures like the noble Bereans.

READ THIS AND PRAY: Send forth your light and your truth, let them guide me; let them bring me to your holy mountain, to the place where you dwell (Psalm 43:3). Sanctify them by the truth; your word is truth (John 17:17).

Prayer: Thank you, Lord, that just as you give preachers their words so you have put a brain between the hearers' ears. Help me to search the Scriptures to see if what I hear in church this Sunday is truly from your Word. Amen.

Maps: Berea; Thessalonica – see pages 126-127
Words: synagogue – see pages 109-113

DAY 27 BIBLE READING
ACTS 17:22-31

²²Paul then stood up in the meeting of the Areopagus and said: "Men of Athens! I see that in every way you are very religious. ²³For as I walked around and looked carefully at your objects of worship, I even found an altar with this inscription: TO AN UNKNOWN GOD. Now what you worship as something unknown I am going to proclaim to you.

²⁴"The God who made the world and everything in it is the Lord of heaven and earth and does not live in temples built by hands. ²⁵And he is not served by human hands, as if he needed anything, because he himself gives all men life and breath and everything else. ²⁶From one man he made every nation of men, that they should inhabit the whole earth; and he determined the times set for them and the exact places where they should live. ²⁷God did this so that men would seek him and perhaps reach out for him and find him, though he is not far from each one of us. ²⁸'For in him we live and move and have our being.' As some of your own poets have said, 'We are his offspring.'

²⁹"Therefore since we are God's offspring, we should not think that the divine being is like gold or silver or stone—an image made by man's design and skill. ³⁰In the past God overlooked such ignorance, but now he commands all people everywhere to repent. ³¹For he has set a day when he will judge the world with justice by the man he has appointed. He has given proof of this to all men by raising him from the dead."

THINK ABOUT YOUR LIFE: Make a list of three people that you know well and who don't know Jesus. Write down what they worry about, what they want to get out of life and what they believe about God. Now ask God to help you tell them what the Bible says about these things.

THINK ABOUT IT: DAY 27
ACTS 17:22-31 ATHENS: THINK ABOUT
THE PEOPLE AROUND YOU

Paul was given an opportunity to speak about the gospel. What did he say to the important and highly educated people who had demanded that he speak?

Well, he'd been very careful as he walked about in Athens to observe the city and its people. He thought very carefully about their lives so that he could find a connection between what he needed to say and what they already thought.

He noticed, as he wandered down a long street with statues and temples and shrines all devoted to as many gods as the citizens could think of, an altar to an unknown god. This was his 'in'! This was how he would find a way into the Athenian world for God's message.

Okay, what are the ways into your friends' worlds for the good news about Jesus? Do you know how folk think, or what they are worried about, or what they are trusting to get them through difficulties or what they want out of life? How does the gospel speak into those things?

READ THIS AND PRAY: I will declare your name to my brothers; in the presence of the congregation I will sing your praises (Hebrews 2:12).

Prayer: Father God, thank you that you have shown us through your Word that you are the one true God. Help me to be able to show my friends and family that you are the only one who can give us the help, love, and satisfaction that our hearts crave. In the name of your Son. Amen.

Maps: Athens – see pages 126-127

DAY 28 BIBLE READING
ACTS 18:1-11

IN CORINTH

¹After this, Paul left Athens and went to Corinth. ²There he met a Jew named Aquila, a native of Pontus, who had recently come from Italy with his wife Priscilla, because Claudius had ordered all the Jews to leave Rome. Paul went to see them, ³and because he was a tentmaker as they were, he stayed and worked with them. ⁴Every Sabbath he reasoned in the synagogue, trying to persuade Jews and Greeks.

⁵When Silas and Timothy came from Macedonia, Paul devoted himself exclusively to preaching, testifying to the Jews that Jesus was the Christ. ⁶But when the Jews opposed Paul and became abusive, he shook out his clothes in protest and said to them, "Your blood be on your own heads! I am clear of my responsibility. From now on I will go to the Gentiles."

⁷Then Paul left the synagogue and went next door to the house of Titius Justus, a worshiper of God. ⁸Crispus, the synagogue ruler, and his entire household believed in the Lord; and many of the Corinthians who heard him believed and were baptized.

⁹One night the Lord spoke to Paul in a vision: "Do not be afraid; keep on speaking, do not be silent. ¹⁰For I am with you, and no one is going to attack and harm you, because I have many people in this city." ¹¹So Paul stayed for a year and a half, teaching them the word of God.

THINK ABOUT IT: DAY 28 ACTS 18:1-11
CORINTH: JESUS AND HIS FRIENDS CAN
HELP YOU

Paul got to pleasure-mad Corinth on his own, bruised and beaten by persecutions, fearful and with no self-confidence at all.

So God sent his weary friend two helpers. He'd never met Priscilla and Aquila before but they were tent-makers like him and they loved Jesus too. They became firm and faithful friends of Paul very quickly.

Then those trusted companions in mission, Timothy and Silas, rejoined Paul with encouraging news about how the churches were doing.

How kind of God to give us good friends who can lift our spirits and hearten us in the mission. But then another friend – the very best friend of all – met up with Paul and gave him fresh courage. Jesus came to him when he was really low and said to him 'Don't be afraid ...' God had already been at work in Corinth. Paul was not alone and would not fail.

What a friend you have in Jesus – the best friend in the whole world.

READ THIS AND PRAY: Be strong and very courageous. Be careful to obey all the law my servant Moses gave you; do not turn from it to the right or to the left, that you may be successful wherever you go (Joshua 1:7).

In God I trust; I will not be afraid. What can man do to me? (Psalm 56:11).

Prayer: Lord Jesus, thank you for my friends, and thank you for being the best friend ever. Help me to be a really good friend who can encourage other believers, just as you do. Give me the courage that I need to stand up for you and for your Word. Amen.

Maps: Corinth; Macedonia – see pages 126-127
Who's Who: Priscilla and Aquila; Claudius; Silas; Timothy – see page 114

DAY 29 BIBLE READING
ACTS 18:19-23

[19]They arrived at Ephesus, where Paul left Priscilla and Aquila. He himself went into the synagogue and reasoned with the Jews. [20]When they asked him to spend more time with them, he declined. [21]But as he left, he promised, "I will come back if it is God's will." Then he set sail from Ephesus. [22]When he landed at Caesarea, he went up and greeted the church and then went down to Antioch.

[23]After spending some time in Antioch, Paul set out from there and travelled from place to place throughout the region of Galatia and Phrygia, strengthening all the disciples.

THINK ABOUT YOUR LIFE: What excites and motivates you most? What are the hopes and dreams that make you work hard, overcome difficulties, solve problems and stick to goals? Does the glory of the name of Jesus appear in your answers? Pray that God will give you a Christ-centred life.

THINK ABOUT IT: DAY 29 ACTS 18:19-23
ALL-CONSUMING PASSION

Luke told the last part of Paul's journey quickly. Soon Paul and his friends were back in the familiar city of Antioch with their old friends and the brothers and sisters in Christ who had sent him and prayed for him.

If we had been in Paul's shoes we'd probably think that we'd earned a good long rest. The journey had been long and demanding in many different ways. Maybe Paul did think about putting his feet up and settling in Antioch. He could have had an easy life there with a fine reputation and plenty of work whenever he wanted it.

But the mission of God was an all-consuming passion for Paul. His heart was fixed on the growth of God's kingdom on earth. Paul's heart had once been so passionate about destroying the name of Jesus but God changed him to a man with a heart for glorifying him.

READ THIS AND PRAY: Do not let this Book of the Law depart from your mouth; meditate on it day and night, so that you may be careful to do everything written in it. Then you will be prosperous and successful (Joshua 1:8).
I can do everything through him who gives me strength. (1 Philippians 4:13).
Whatever you do, work at it with all your heart, as working for the Lord, not for men (Colossians 3:23).

Prayer: Dear Lord and Father, give me a passion for your Word and your kingdom. May my life be dedicated to your glory. May Christ be the centre of my life. Amen.

Maps: Antioch; Galatia; Phrygia; Ephesus; Caesarea – see pages 126-127
Words: glorify; kingdom – see pages 109-113

PART 6

PAUL'S THIRD MISSIONARY JOURNEY – HOW TO STRENGTHEN OTHER BELIEVERS

Not everything in God's mission is about making new believers. Some of it is about God's work of helping people who are already Christians to be strong and to keep following Jesus closely. It's not just in God's heart to strengthen believers. If our hearts are full of God's love for people then we will naturally want to help them too.

Paul's third journey was mostly spent going round the churches that he'd planted or that had been started by folk who became Christians through the preaching of some of God's other missionaries.

You can see on the map on page 127 where he went and as we follow Paul over the next five days we see how God used him to make the fellowships in these places stronger. This will be a brilliant guide to help you help other Christians wherever God has put you today. So instead of becoming one of those 'high-maintenance' Christians who only thinks about what other people should do for them, be a loving Christian, who thinks far more about what you can do for your brothers and sisters in Jesus.

You'll need to read Acts 18:23–20:38 to get the whole story – it won't take long so why not do it just now?

Part 6
Acts 18:23 – 20: 38
Paul's Third Journey:
How to Strengthen Other Believers

DAY 30 BIBLE READING

ACTS 19:8-20

⁸Paul entered the synagogue and spoke boldly there for three months, arguing persuasively about the kingdom of God. ⁹But some of them became obstinate; they refused to believe and publicly maligned the Way. So Paul left them. He took the disciples with him and had discussions daily in the lecture hall of Tyrannus. ¹⁰This went on for two years, so that all the Jews and Greeks who lived in the province of Asia heard the word of the Lord.

¹¹God did extraordinary miracles through Paul, ¹²so that even handkerchiefs and aprons that had touched him were taken to the sick, and their illnesses were cured and the evil spirits left them.

¹³Some Jews who went around driving out evil spirits tried to invoke the name of the Lord Jesus over those who were demon-possessed. They would say, "In the name of Jesus, whom Paul preaches, I command you to come out." ¹⁴Seven sons of Sceva, a Jewish chief priest, were doing this. ¹⁵(One day) the evil spirit answered them, "Jesus I know, and I know about Paul, but who are you?" ¹⁶Then the man who had the evil spirit jumped on them and overpowered them all. He gave them such a beating that they ran out of the house naked and bleeding.

¹⁷When this became known to the Jews and Greeks living in Ephesus, they were all seized with fear, and the name of the Lord Jesus was held in high honour. ¹⁸Many of those who believed now came and openly confessed their evil deeds. ¹⁹A number who had practiced sorcery brought their scrolls together and burned them publicly. When they calculated the value of the scrolls, the total came to fifty thousand drachmas. ²⁰In this way the word of the Lord spread widely and grew in power.

Maps: Ephesus – see pages 126-127
Words: miracles – see pages 109-113

Think about it: DAY 30 Acts 19:8-20
Ephesus: Help the church to grow

Ephesus is a set of ruins nowadays. It's in Turkey and thousands of tourists flock to it every year. In Paul's day it was a large, wealthy city with many temples dedicated to many gods. There were already believers there when Paul arrived but he wanted to see the church grow and reach more people with the gospel.

So how did he help them? Well, it involved the following:

1.   The Spirit giving his power
2.   God's Word being taught
3.   Convincing evidence that Jesus is God's King and
4.   People getting rid of bad things in their lives.

Think about the place you live. Would you like to see the number of believers grow there? If you would, who can you ask the Lord to help, so that the same things happen in your town or village or city? You might think of praying for your Pastor and other leaders in the church. You might also start to pray for all the believers where you live. It might even be that you need to say 'Lord, here I am; use me to help your church to grow here.'

READ THIS AND PRAY: I heard the voice of the Lord saying, "Whom shall I send? And who will go for us?" And I said, "Here am I. Send me!" (Isaiah 6:8).

"They will be mine," says the LORD Almighty, "in the day when I make up my treasured possession. I will spare them, just as in compassion a man spares his son who serves him. And you will again see the distinction between the righteous and the wicked, between those who serve God and those who do not" (Malachi 3:17-18).

Prayer: Lord, thank you that even I can be helpful on your mission. Please use me as you want, wherever you put me and whenever you want. You have put me here now, so please use me today to help your church to grow. Amen.

DAY 31 BIBLE READING
ACTS 20:1-6

THROUGH MACEDONIA AND GREECE

[1]When the uproar had ended, Paul sent for the disciples and, after encouraging them, said goodbye and set out for Macedonia. [2]He travelled through that area, speaking many words of encouragement to the people, and finally arrived in Greece, [3]where he stayed three months. Because the Jews made a plot against him just as he was about to sail for Syria, he decided to go back through Macedonia. [4]He was accompanied by Sopater son of Pyrrhus from Berea, Aristarchus and Secundus from Thessalonica, Gaius from Derbe, Timothy also, and Tychicus and Trophimus from the province of Asia. [5]These men went on ahead and waited for us at Troas. [6]But we sailed from Philippi after the Feast of Unleavened Bread, and five days later joined the others at Troas, where we stayed seven days.

MISSIONARY JOURNEYS: Paul travelled a lot and went on several journeys – at least three of which are referred to as missionary journeys. You read about his first journey in Acts 13:4–14:28; his second in Acts 15:40–18:23; his third in Acts 18:23–20:38. There is a fourth journey that he does under arrest as he is taken to trial in Rome.

Maps: Philippi – see pages 126-127

Think about it: DAY 31 Acts 20:1-6
Macedonia and Greece: Work with
them for god

This book should really be called '40 Days with Paul and his Companions'!

We often talk about Paul's missionary journeys or Paul planting churches. But really it was Paul and a lot of others. He didn't believe in doing it all by himself. He needed other people: in fact he was dependent on them. This is interesting because it tells you that independence is not a sign of maturity but immaturity. And independence is not effective in the work of God in this world. It's nearly useless.

You must learn to work with other people in the church even if they are different from you – older or younger, coming from a different background or even a different country. You need to be patient and kind and you need to trust them. It's not easy! And they will need to do the same with you. It's about being part of a team: God's team in the place where you live.

READ THIS AND PRAY: Glorify the LORD with me; let us exalt his name together (Psalm 34:33).

For where two or three come together in my name, there am I with them (Matthew 18:20).

My purpose is that they may be encouraged in heart and united in love, so that they may have the full riches of complete understanding, in order that they may know the mystery of God, namely, Christ (Colossians 2:2).

Prayer: Lord, help me to work well with others; may my time with them be an encouragement to them and make a difference in their lives. Help us together to make an impact for Jesus in our community. Amen.

DAY 32 BIBLE READING
ACTS 20:7-12

EUTYCHUS RAISED FROM THE DEAD AT TROAS

[7]On the first day of the week we came together to break bread. Paul spoke to the people and, because he intended to leave the next day, kept on talking until midnight. [8]There were many lamps in the upstairs room where we were meeting. [9]Seated in a window was a young man named Eutychus, who was sinking into a deep sleep as Paul talked on and on. When he was sound asleep, he fell to the ground from the third story and was picked up dead. [10]Paul went down, threw himself on the young man and put his arms around him. "Don't be alarmed," he said. "He's alive!" [11]Then he went upstairs again and broke bread and ate. After talking until daylight, he left. [12]The people took the young man home alive and were greatly comforted.

PAUL'S WRITINGS: Many of the books in the New Testament are written by Paul. He wrote the following epistles or letters to different churches that he had visited during his journeys – as well as to some individuals. Here is a list of the books in the Bible that are written by Paul: Romans; 1 & 2 Corinthians; Galatians; Ephesians; Philippians; Colossians; 1 & 2 Thessalonians; 1 & 2 Timothy; Titus; Philemon and possibly Hebrews too.

Who's Who: Eutychus; Luke – see page 114
Maps: Troas – see pages 126-127

Think about it: DAY 32 Acts 20:7-12
Troas: be hungry for God's word

What an amazing night that was in Troas! I suppose that Eutychus never forgot it for the rest of his life. The astonishing thing is that such a remarkable miracle wasn't the main thing on everyone's mind. Do you notice what Luke tells us? Paul preached for a long time, well into the night, and yet after Eutychus was raised from the dead the Christians went back and listened to more until dawn. They were more hungry for the Word of God than they were for miracles! They must have had a deep sense that they needed to be taught and that it was more important than the normal routines of life and even of the immediate needs of their bodies for sleep and food.

It could never be normal, but that night in Troas does make us ask a question: Do I always want food and rest more than God's Word? Is there never a time when I want to put the normal routines of life to one side for the sake of hearing what God has to say through his Word?

READ THIS AND PRAY: Blessed are those who hunger and thirst for righteousness, for they will be filled (Matthew 5:6). For he satisfies the thirsty and fills the hungry with good things (Psalm 107:9).

Prayer: Heavenly Father, please give me a hunger for your Word that demands to be satisfied more loudly and urgently than the demands of my other appetites. I remember what your Son has said: that man shall not live by bread alone but by every Word that has come from your mouth. Help me not to neglect my spiritual hunger. Amen.

Words: Miracle; Righteousness – see pages 109-113

DAY 33 BIBLE READING
Acts 20:32-38

[32]"Now I commit you to God and to the word of his grace, which can build you up and give you an inheritance among all those who are sanctified. [33]I have not coveted anyone's silver or gold or clothing. [34]You yourselves know that these hands of mine have supplied my own needs and the needs of my companions. [35]In everything I did, I showed you that by this kind of hard work we must help the weak, remembering the words the Lord Jesus himself said: 'It is more blessed to give than to receive.' "

[36]When he had said this, he knelt down with all of them and prayed. [37]They all wept as they embraced him and kissed him. [38]What grieved them most was his statement that they would never see his face again. Then they accompanied him to the ship.

WHAT IS LOVE? Is love just hearts and flowers and romance? Is it to do with having a best friend who would do anything for you? Is it to do with the love that a parent has for a child? These are all different kinds of love – romantic love, friendship love and parental love. But there is a greater love than these – that is the love of God. Love is more than emotion. The Bible often describes love with active words. If you read 1 Corinthians 13 you will read that love is patient and kind and does not envy. It isn't proud. It doesn't boast. That's a tall order, isn't it? But we have the help of the Lord Jesus Christ. He is the greatest example of what true love is. John 3:16 says that God so loved the world that he sent his only Son so that whoever believes in him should not perish but have everlasting life. 1 John 3:16 tells us that we can know what love is because Jesus laid down his life for us.

THINK ABOUT IT: DAY 33 ACTS 20:32-38
MILETUS: LOVE YOUR FELLOW-BELIEVERS

We're given a glimpse of something very precious in today's reading: love. We've seen how Paul preached and how he suffered. We've seen how he planted churches, whatever the cost. But the Bible says that the greatest thing to have in our hearts and in our church is love. Paul loved the Ephesian Christians so deeply that he was never selfish or wanted their money, he worked hard not to be a burden to them, he wanted to help them in every way that he could. And when the elders of the church realised that this was the last time they would see him they were moved to tears, so great was their love for him.

It's right to want your church to be good at the activities that it's supposed be doing, but it is so important that your church becomes a place of love. Love is more important than busyness or being up-to-date with music or having big numbers. Aim for love and you will be aiming for the heart of God to be revealed among you in your fellowship.

READ THIS AND PRAY: Because your love is better than life, my lips will glorify you (Psalm 63:3).

Now that you have purified yourselves by obeying the truth so that you have sincere love for your brothers, love one another deeply, from the heart (1 Peter 1:22).

The entire law is summed up in a single command: "Love your neighbour as yourself" (Galatians 5:14).

Prayer: Thank you, Lord, for your loving kindness to me. Help me to show that love to my brothers and sisters in my church. Help us to be a place where whatever we've done and whoever we are, we know that we are loved. Amen.

DAY 34 BIBLE READING
Acts 20:20-24

20You know that I have not hesitated to preach anything that would be helpful to you, but have taught you publicly and from house to house. 21I have declared to both Jews and Greeks that they must turn to God in repentance and have faith in our Lord Jesus.

22"And now, compelled by the Spirit, I am going to Jerusalem, not knowing what will happen to me there. 23I only know that in every city the Holy Spirit warns me that prison and hardships are facing me. 24However, I consider my life worth nothing to me, if only I may finish the race and complete the task the Lord Jesus has given me—the task of testifying to the gospel of God's grace."

THE RACE: This is a good way to describe the Christian life. If you've ever been in a race you will know that it can be hard going sometimes. It's the same when you live as a Christian. It's not easy. When you run in a race you have to focus on the finishing line. Christians have to focus on the final goal of their lives which is heaven – being with Christ. That is our final destination. Keep up the pace. Keep on going. Don't give up. The race is worth running. Jesus is worth it all.

JEWISH CEREMONIAL LAWS: These were laws and rituals that the Jewish people were instructed to keep as they were pointing towards the coming of the Lord Jesus Christ, the Messiah. After the Messiah had come and had fulfilled the law, taking the punishment for sin, these laws and rituals were no longer required.

THINK ABOUT IT: DAY 34 ACTS 20:20-24
JERUSALEM: PUT OTHERS FIRST

When Paul's third journey was over he got back to Jerusalem. He already knew that he would be arrested at some point and would have to suffer for the gospel. But the gospel was more important to Paul than his own comfort or his own way of doing things.

So when an obstacle was getting in the way of Jews becoming Christians or growing in their faith, Paul put other people and their obedience to the gospel before his own preferences. He didn't need to do what was asked of him. He had turned away from the Jewish ceremonial laws. But for the sake of the gospel and others, he did what was asked and took part in the duties that went with a vow that others had made. It wasn't a sin to do these things so he put others first and adapted what he would normally have preferred to do.

So next time you're asked to give something up that God allows you to do, consider giving it up anyway for the sake of other people and to make the gospel of Jesus shine more clearly.

READ THIS AND PRAY: For by the grace given me I say to every one of you: Do not think of yourself more highly than you ought, but rather think of yourself with sober judgment, in accordance with the measure of faith God has given you (Romans 12:3).

Therefore God exalted him to the highest place and gave him the name that is above every name, that at the name of Jesus every knee should bow, in heaven and on earth and under the earth, and every tongue confess that Jesus Christ is Lord, to the glory of God the Father (Philippians 2:9-11).

Prayer: Forgive me, Lord, for the times that I've just dug my heels in and not done what others want me to do just because I've been stubborn and selfish. Please help me to be as humble as Paul was here. Amen.

PART 7

Paul's fourth journey: be faithful to God all the way

We sometimes think that if we are doing what God wants us to do life will be easy. But for thousands of believers around the world today, being on God's mission is costly. It costs them their jobs, or their freedom; sometimes it costs them their lives.

As Paul was making his way back to Jerusalem on the third journey, he was told by the Holy Spirit (we don't know how he was told so it's no use guessing) that he was going to suffer. While he was in prison in Jerusalem, Jesus came to him and told him that he would go to Rome to be a witness there.

The fourth journey that we follow is the journey from Jerusalem to Rome. It wasn't a missionary journey in the way that the others had been, but Paul still told people about Jesus while he travelled. He was still on God's mission. On this journey Paul experienced again and again the fulfilling of Jesus' promise that he would be with his followers all the time, everywhere they went, whoever they met and whatever they had to do.

As well as looking at the map, you'll need to read a big chunk of Acts, from 21:17 to the end of the book. But it's a gripping story and all the more so because it's true.

PART 7

ACTS 21:17 – 28:31

PAUL'S FOURTH JOURNEY: BE FAITHFUL TO GOD
ALL THE WAY

DAY 35 BIBLE READING

LUKE 12:4-12 & 22-26

⁴"I tell you, my friends, do not be afraid of those who kill the body and after that can do no more. ⁵But I will show you whom you should fear: Fear him who, after the killing of the body, has power to throw you into hell. Yes, I tell you, fear him. ⁶Are not five sparrows sold for two pennies? Yet not one of them is forgotten by God. ⁷Indeed, the very hairs of your head are all numbered. Don't be afraid; you are worth more than many sparrows.

⁸"I tell you, whoever acknowledges me before men, the Son of Man will also acknowledge him before the angels of God. ⁹But he who disowns me before men will be disowned before the angels of God. ¹⁰And everyone who speaks a word against the Son of Man will be forgiven, but anyone who blasphemes against the Holy Spirit will not be forgiven.

¹¹"When you are brought before synagogues, rulers and authorities, do not worry about how you will defend yourselves or what you will say, ¹²for the Holy Spirit will teach you at that time what you should say."

²²Then Jesus said to his disciples: "Therefore I tell you, do not worry about your life, what you will eat; or about your body, what you will wear. ²³Life is more than food, and the body more than clothes. ²⁴Consider the ravens: They do not sow or reap, they have no storeroom or barn; yet God feeds them. And how much more valuable you are than birds! ²⁵Who of you by worrying can add a single hour to his life? ²⁶Since you cannot do this very little thing, why do you worry about the rest?"

THINK ABOUT IT: DAY 35
LUKE 12:4-12 & 22-26
ARRESTED IN CAESAREA: JESUS KEEPS
HIS PROMISE

You'll have read what else happened in Jerusalem after yesterday's reading. Now Paul found himself in Caesarea and on trial again for his faith. He was among some very sharp lawyers and powerful men. What did he say?

Well, Jesus knew that those who followed him would face what he faced. He was hauled before the rulers of Jerusalem, put on trial and beaten. And he said that would happen to his followers. So he made a promise. He said that whenever that happened, God would send the Holy Spirit to teach his followers what to say. The Spirit would give the right ideas and the right words so that the message would be heard clearly. A calm heart and a clear head and a careful tongue would come from the Spirit's helpful, though unseen, presence. So when Paul spoke so well in Caesarea it was because the Spirit was there, and the Spirit was there because Jesus was keeping his promise. HE always will, so don't be afraid when you have to speak for Jesus. He will help you as much as you need.

READ THIS AND PRAY: My tongue will speak of your righteousness and of your praises all day long (Psalm 35:28).

But when they arrest you, do not worry about what to say or how to say it. At that time you will be given what to say, for it will not be you speaking, but the Spirit of your Father speaking through you (Matthew 10:19-20).

Prayer: Thank you, Lord, that you are always near to help me. Please teach me to trust you to be with me. I know that you can help me to speak boldly and clearly about Jesus. Help me especially when I think that I don't need you! Amen.

Words: Forgiven; Holy Spirit – see pages 109-113
For persecution see Think Spots on page 72

DAY 36 BIBLE READING
ACTS 26:28-32

28Then Agrippa said to Paul, "Do you think that in such a short time you can persuade me to be a Christian?"

29Paul replied, "Short time or long—I pray God that not only you but all who are listening to me today may become what I am, except for these chains."

30The king rose, and with him the governor and Bernice and those sitting with them. 31They left the room, and while talking with one another, they said, "This man is not doing anything that deserves death or imprisonment."

32Agrippa said to Festus, "This man could have been set free if he had not appealed to Caesar."

YOUR SOUL: Your soul is so valuable you can never put a price on it. It is so precious that there is nothing that you could exchange for it. You have a soul that is more valuable than the world itself. The Bible says that the soul that sins shall die but your soul can be saved from sin by Jesus Christ. Eternal life for your soul is only obtained through believing in Jesus. Your soul and resurrected body will live forever with Christ if you believe in him. If you don't believe, your soul and resurrected body will die forever in eternal punishment.

THINK ABOUT IT: DAY 36 ACTS 26:28-32 BEFORE WICKED LEADERS: SOME PEOPLE COULDN'T CARE LESS!

We know that the gospel is the most important message in the world. But some of the people that God sends you among just don't see it that way. Festus and Agrippa and Bernice were like that.

The really sad thing is that even though they had heard Paul speak clearly, they really didn't care about what he had been saying. When they walked away, in verse 32, they weren't talking to each other about the love of God for them, or about their need to repent of their sin, or about Jesus and the cross. They were talking about the legal process to be carried out. The gospel meant nothing to them and had no impact on them. They really couldn't care less.

Apathy has taken more people to hell than blatant wickedness. Don't be surprised when some of the people around you couldn't care less about their souls. And don't let your own heart get like that.

READ THIS AND PRAY: Only be careful, and watch yourselves closely so that you do not forget the things your eyes have seen or let them slip from your heart as long as you live. Teach them to your children and to their children after them (Deuteronomy 4:9)
What good will it be for a man if he gains the whole world, yet forfeits his soul? Or what can a man give in exchange for his soul? (Matthew 16:26).

Prayer: Lord, please help me to care about my soul and the souls of those around me – even if that means I care about them more than they care about themselves. Penetrate the armour of apathy with which some of the people around me defend themselves from the attack of the gospel. Amen.

Words: soul – see pages 109-113
Boot Camp 001/Getting started with you – hell – see page 116
Who's Who: Agrippa; Festus; Caesar – see page 114

DAY 37 BIBLE READING
Acts 27:21-26

[21]After the men had gone a long time without food, Paul stood up before them and said: "Men, you should have taken my advice not to sail from Crete; then you would have spared yourselves this damage and loss. [22]But now I urge you to keep up your courage, because not one of you will be lost; only the ship will be destroyed. [23]Last night an angel of the God whose I am and whom I serve stood beside me [24]and said, 'Do not be afraid, Paul. You must stand trial before Caesar; and God has graciously given you the lives of all who sail with you.' [25]So keep up your courage, men, for I have faith in God that it will happen just as he told me. [26]Nevertheless, we must run aground on some island."

THINK ABOUT YOUR LIFE: Which Christians have you really admired for their leadership? Thank God for them, pray for them, and write down what it was that made them such effective leaders. Ask God to give you that kind of character.

THINK ABOUT IT: DAY 37 ACTS 27:21-26
ALL AT SEA: BEING A LEADER IN A CRISIS

It's difficult when no one listens to you, isn't it? You can get really annoyed. It's such a temptation to let people try and find their own way out of the disaster that you'd seen coming. Paul saw a disaster waiting to happen but instead of being huffy, Paul took command and lead people to safety. Here's how:

He commanded their attention.

He established that he was worth listening to.

He put courage in their fearful hearts.

He gave them a message from God.

He told them that it was not going to be easy.

Later (verses 33-38) he told them to be sensible and eat something and he led by example.

Do the same when others are losing their nerve in a crisis. Believe God, stay calm and help others out of their desperation or their panic. The bit about believing God is the key. If you want to keep your head, keep your eyes on Jesus!

READ THIS AND PRAY: Be strong and courageous. Do not be afraid or terrified because of them, for the LORD your God goes with you; he will never leave you nor forsake you (Deuteronomy 31:6).

Wait for the LORD; be strong and take heart and wait for the LORD (Psalm 27:14).

Prayer: Father God, help me to focus on you in times of prosperity and in times of hardship. May I keep calm in the crisis and thankful during the good times, because I trust in you. Give me the strength of character to lead others when they are in distress. In the name of your Son. Amen.

DAY 38 BIBLE READING

Acts 28:11-14

ARRIVAL AT ROME

¹¹After three months we put out to sea in a ship that had wintered in the island. It was an Alexandrian ship with the figurehead of the twin gods Castor and Pollux. ¹²We put in at Syracuse and stayed there three days. ¹³From there we set sail and arrived at Rhegium. The next day the south wind came up, and on the following day we reached Puteoli. ¹⁴There we found some brothers who invited us to spend a week with them. And so we came to Rome.

READ THIS: In my Father's house are many rooms; if it were not so, I would have told you. I am going there to prepare a place for you. And if I go and prepare a place for you, I will come back and take you to be with me that you also may be where I am (John 14:2-3).

THINK ABOUT IT: DAY 38 ACTS 28:11-14
SAFE ARRIVAL: WHO GETS YOU THROUGH
LIFE'S JOURNEYS?

It wasn't those false gods Castor and Pollux who got them all safely to Rome, was it? It was the living God of heaven and earth!

And who will get you and me safely through life's missionary journey to heaven? It won't be 'luck' or 'fortune'; it won't be the modern gods of 'self-sufficiency' or 'status'. It will be the same living God of heaven and earth!

The world trusts itself and, of course, gives itself all the credit when things go well. But when we get to heaven we'll see who got us there. We'll give all the credit to Jesus Christ as we praise and worship him with his people. They'll all be there – safely home from every tribe and language and nation and tongue. You can thank him now that he will see you safely home.

READ THIS AND PRAY: Who shall separate us from the love of Christ? Shall trouble or hardship or persecution or famine or nakedness or danger or sword? As it is written: "For your sake we face death all day long; we are considered as sheep to be slaughtered." No, in all these things we are more than conquerors through him who loved us. For I am convinced that neither death nor life, neither angels nor demons, neither the present nor the future, nor any powers, neither height nor depth, nor anything else in all creation, will be able to separate us from the love of God that is in Christ Jesus our Lord (Romans 8:35-39).

Prayer: Heavenly Father, I thank you that Jesus has gone ahead to prepare a place for me in your eternal house, which is my true home. Give me faith to trust you and a heart to praise you. Thank you that nothing can separate me from your love which is mine forever in Jesus. Amen.

DAY 39 BIBLE READING
Acts 28:30-31

³⁰For two whole years Paul stayed there in his own rented house and welcomed all who came to see him. ³¹Boldly and without hindrance he preached the kingdom of God and taught about the Lord Jesus Christ.

Colossians 4:2-5
²Devote yourselves to prayer, being watchful and thankful. ³And pray for us, too, that God may open a door for our message, so that we may proclaim the mystery of Christ, for which I am in chains. ⁴Pray that I may proclaim it clearly, as I should. ⁵Be wise in the way you act toward outsiders; make the most of every opportunity.

PERSEVERE: It can be difficult to keep going during hard and stressful times. Here are some verses, however, in the Bible that talk about perseverance and how important it is.

You need to persevere so that when you have done the will of God, you will receive what he has promised (Hebrews 10:36).

Blessed is the man who perseveres under trial, because when he has stood the test, he will receive the crown of life that God has promised to those who love him (James 1:12).

Watch your life and doctrine closely. Persevere in them, because if you do, you will save both yourself and your hearers (1 Timothy 4:16).

THINK ABOUT IT: DAY 39 ACTS 28:30-31;
COLOSSIANS 4:2-5
PAUL IN ROME: NEVER STOP SERVING GOD

Jesus had said to Paul that he would go to Rome to testify there (see Acts 22:11). So what did Paul do when he got there? He started on the work of God's mission, even though he was under house arrest. He talked to the Jews about Jesus to try to convince them about Jesus. Many would not listen but that didn't put him off – it never did! So for two years he went on boldly preaching that Jesus is the King and Saviour. Paul did not stop serving God.

Do you remember what I wrote at the beginning of this book? Every day that God gives is a day for his mission – there's no other reason for today, even though there are many things to enjoy in it.

So don't give up! Persevere! As long as there is a day called 'today' then it's a day to take part in the wonderful mission that God is on.

READ THIS AND PRAY: Turn to me and have mercy on me; grant your strength to your servant and save the son of your maidservant (Psalm 86:16).

"Do not grieve, for the joy of the LORD is your strength" (Nehemiah 8:10).
And the God of all grace, who called you to his eternal glory in Christ, after you have suffered a little while, will himself restore you and make you strong, firm and steadfast (1 Peter 5:10).

Prayer: Lord, sometimes I get tired in your work, but please never let me get tired of your work. Thank you that this day you want me to join with you on your mission of grace and mercy in this world with which you are so patient. Amen.

Maps: Rome – see page 127

DAY 40 BIBLE READING
2 TIMOTHY 3:10-17

¹⁰You, however, know all about my teaching, my way of life, my purpose, faith, patience, love, endurance, ¹¹persecutions, sufferings—what kinds of things happened to me in Antioch, Iconium and Lystra, the persecutions I endured. Yet the Lord rescued me from all of them. ¹²In fact, everyone who wants to live a godly life in Christ Jesus will be persecuted, ¹³while evil men and impostors will go from bad to worse, deceiving and being deceived. ¹⁴But as for you, continue in what you have learned and have become convinced of, because you know those from whom you learned it, ¹⁵and how from infancy you have known the holy Scriptures, which are able to make you wise for salvation through faith in Christ Jesus. ¹⁶All Scripture is God-breathed and is useful for teaching, rebuking, correcting and training in righteousness, ¹⁷so that the man of God may be thoroughly equipped for every good work.

READ THIS AND PRAY: Store up for yourselves treasures in heaven, where moth and rust do not destroy, and where thieves do not break in and steal. For where your treasure is, there your heart will be also (Matthew 6 20-21).

Prayer: Lord God, help me to realise what is truly precious – your Word, your name and salvation. Teach me to value these above all else. In the name of your Son Jesus Christ. Amen.

BROTHERS AND SISTERS: When you trust in Christ to save you from your sin you become part of God's family. You can call God 'Father' – just as Jesus does. Jesus is your elder brother in God's family. All other believers are your spiritual siblings – brothers and sisters in Jesus Christ.

Think about it: DAY 40
2 Timothy 3:10-17
top tips for missionaries

On our last day with Paul I want to highlight eight aspects of his life that we need God's help to put into practice. This checklist will show you where you need God's help and where God has been at work in your life. It will also show you ways to pray for your brothers and sisters in Jesus – your fellow-missionaries – all over the world and where you live.

It's been great to share these past forty days with you. May the Lord Jesus help you to run with patience and joy the course that he sets out for you as you share his mission with him.

1. Use the best tool for God's mission: God's Word. Read it, learn it, do it, pass it on. (2 Timothy 3:14-17)
2. Honour God with courageously faithful witness and stick at it. Don't quit: Jesus didn't. (Acts 20:24)
3. Put aside your own preferences for the sake of other people coming to know Jesus. (1 Corinthians 9:22)
4. Watch out for the devil, particularly in the good times. (1 Timothy 4:16)
5. Fix your mind and heart on heaven: it will help you to endure troubles on earth! (2 Corinthians 4:18)
6. Don't get proud about yourself; be really proud of Jesus. (1 Corinthians 1: 28-31)
7. Work together with others and strengthen one another in love. (Ephesians 4:16)
8. Trust God's promises: make decisions about your life, believing that God will do what he has promised to do. (Romans 15:13)

PAUL'S MINISTRY

FIRST JOURNEY – INTO GALATIA
AD 46 to 48 (Acts 13 and 14)

Planted churches in: Pisidian Antioch; Iconium; Lystra; Derbe; Perga
Wrote nothing!

SECOND JOURNEY – INTO GREECE
AD 49 to 52 (Acts 15:40 to 18:22)

Planted churches in: Philippi; Thessalonica; Berea; Athens; Corinth; Ephesus
Wrote: 1 & 2 Thessalonians (from Corinth)

THIRD JOURNEY – ROUND THE AEGEAN
AD 53 to 58 (Acts 18:23 to 20:38)

Revisited many churches including Thessalonica (Acts 20:1-3)
Wrote: Galatians (from Ephesus); 1 Corinthians (from Ephesus); 2 Corinthians (from Macedonia); Romans (from Corinth)

IMPRISONMENT IN CAESAREA THEN ROME
AD 59 to 63 (Acts 21:17 to 28)

Wrote: Philippians; Ephesians; Colossians; Philemon (from prison in Rome)

PROBABLY A FINAL JOURNEY
AD 63 (?) to 67 (starting point is Acts 28:30)

Visited Crete and Macedonia; re-imprisoned and martyred in Rome
Wrote: 1 Timothy; Titus; 2 Timothy (from prison in Rome)

WORDS

Believe: Believing in God means that you are convinced about the truth of God and therefore you are trusting yourself to him in faith. You have accepted Jesus Christ as your personal Saviour.

Blessed: This means to be made holy or to be made very happy and given great gifts.

Church: It is a group of people who follow Jesus. The Church of Christ is in many countries around the world. It is growing every day. It is also a building that people worship God in.

Confess: To admit to doing something wrong. We can confess our sin to God and he is faithful and just and will forgive us our sins.

Converted: This is when someone has their opinion or belief changed.

Creator: The name given to God in his role as the maker of all things.

Crucified: This is what happened to Jesus when he was hung on the cross and left to die. Crucifixion was a method of execution in Roman times.

Devil: The name of God's enemy. Also known as Satan or the tempter.

Disciple: The name given to a person who follows someone. The group of twelve men that Jesus chose as his particular companions were his twelve disciples.

Envy: This is a feeling of discontent that is brought on by desiring someone else's possessions, talents or achievements.

Eternal/Eternity: Eternal means never having had a beginning and never having an end. This is what God is like. He is eternal. We are created by God so we aren't eternal like he is. Our lives in this world are limited by time. God created time for us. We had a beginning when we were conceived and our lives here will end when we die. Eternity has no such limits. It had no beginning and it will have no end. It is infinite. This is impossible for us to fully understand but the Bible teaches us that when we die we too will be in eternity. Our souls and resurrected bodies will live eternally in heaven or die eternally in hell. These are solemn thoughts but it is amazing that when we trust completely in what the Lord Jesus Christ has done and understand who he is we can look forward to enjoying eternity with God in heaven forever.

Faith: Faith is a word used to describe believing in God and Jesus Christ. The Bible describes faith as being certain of what you do not see. Though we can't see God we know he is real, we know his Word is true and faithful and that we can trust in the Lord Jesus Christ to save us from sin. This is faith.

Faithful: This means completely trustworthy. We can always rely on God to do the right thing, the just thing, he is perfect and holy; we can depend on him. He is faithful.

Fasting: To go without food for a period of time. In the Bible Christians prayed and fasted and sometimes Christians still do.

Father: God is our heavenly Father. He is everything that a Father should be. Earthly fathers fail us – but God never fails us.

Forgive/Forgiven: This is when God looks on our sin and instead of punishing us as we deserve he blots out our sin and accepts us into his family because of Christ's death on the cross for us.

Gentile: This was a name given to someone who was not a Jew. A Jew belongs to the Jewish people. A Gentile is someone belonging to any of the other people groups or nations.

Glorify: This means to give honour and praise to someone. We should glorify God – we should show that we love him and follow him. Nothing we do or say should bring dishonour to God.

Gospel: This means good news. The gospel of Jesus Christ is good news because he has saved his people from their sins. The first four books of the New Testament are specifically called Gospels – The Gospel of Matthew, Mark, Luke and John.

Grace: God's grace is generous, wonderful, amazing and free. This is what grace is – all the wonderful things that God gives us such as eternal life, freedom from sin, heaven, love, joy, peace! Everything we need and more! This is his abundant, free grace. Grace is when God gives us what we don't deserve. We deserve death and eternal punishment but through Christ's death on the cross God gives all those who believe in him eternal life.

Heaven: This is where those who believe in Jesus as their saviour will go when they die. God is there and will take his people to be with him for all eternity. The souls of believers go to be with the Lord at the moment of their death. On the Day of Judgement our risen, perfect bodies will be reunited with our souls in heaven.

Jews: The Jews were described as God's chosen people. Today God's chosen people come from not just one tribe but from many tribes and nations and languages.

Kingdom: God's kindgom is the earth and heaven and everthing that is in this world and beyond this world. His people are being added to his kingdom day by day.

Mercy: This is compassion towards an offender or enemy. God shows mercy to sinners who because of their sin are his enemies.

Messiah (Christ): Means Promised One. God promised a Saviour in the Old Testament and Jesus is the fulfilment of that promise.

Miracle/Miracles: This is a word for the amazing supernatural acts that Jesus performed such as healing the sick, giving sight to the blind, feeding five thousand people and walking on the water.

Mission: A specific task assigned to a person or group; a task or duty that a person believes he or she must achieve. God gives his people the mission of glorifying him and spreading the good news of Jesus Christ to others.

Praise: This is when we tell God how wonderful he is and how we are thankful for who he is and what he has done for us

Preach: This word means to tell others about the good news of Jesus Christ, to teach people about God, and to explain God's Word to them. Preaching is a very important part of the life of the church.

Pride: A feeling of satisfaction over your achievements. An overly high opinion of yourself. We should not feel pride in ourselves. All the good things that we do are because of God. Without him we would be nothing.

Prophet: A person chosen by God to pass on his message.

Repent/Repentance: This is when someone is sorry for their sin and turns away from it, turning to God instead to forgive their sins and to help them live a righteous life in the future.

Righteous/Righteousness: God is righteous. To be righteous means to be like God – without sin. We can be righteous only because of Jesus. If we turn to him he will cover us with his righteousness. There is nothing in us that is righteous.

Salvation: This is when Jesus saves his people from their sin. It is what we receive when we repent of our sin and turn back to God.

Satan: See Devil.

Saviour: The name given to Jesus as he came to save his people from their sins.

Sin: Anything that we do, say or think that is against God's commands. Anything that we fail to do, say or think that God commands us.

Sinners: All human beings are sinners. Jesus Christ was the only one who was born without sin. From the moment they are conceived they are born into a life of sin. From the time of Adam's first sin all humanity have been born with a sinful nature. The only one who can conquer and who has conquered sin, is Jesus Christ through his death on the cross.

Soul: God breathed into Adam (the first man) the breath of life and Adam became a living soul. You have a soul too – you aren't just a body. Your soul will last forever – either in heaven or in hell. Our bodies will too after they are resurrected. God tells us in his Word that we are to love the Lord our God with all our heart, soul and mind (Matthew 22:37).

Sovereign/Sovereignty: This is used to describe God's absolute power and authority over all creation, mankind and everything that happens. Nothing happens without his knowledge. He is in control. He knows what is for the best and even when bad things happen we can trust him. He is all powerful.

Synagogue: This was the local place of prayer and worship for Jews in Bible times. They would meet there to worship on the Sabbath and at other times. Jews still do.

The Temple: This was the place of worship in Jerusalem. People would go there to offer sacrifices to God of young lambs or pigeons. The temple was divided into different areas. One area was called the Most Holy Place. This was where the High Priest went each year to seek forgiveness from God for the sins of the people. This day was the Day of Atonement.

Temptation: This is something that prompts desire in us to do what is against God's law. Jesus knows what it is like to be tempted. He was tempted by the devil. The difference between Jesus and us is that we often give into temptation. He never did. Jesus is sinless.

Testimony: This means a story or account of facts. If you give a testimony you are telling others about something that has happened. Christians are told to give an account or testimony of how God has helped them and saved them from sin.

Wisdom: The ability to make the right decisons and judgements through knowledge of and obedience to God's Word.

Witness: Someone who can give first-hand evidence of an event. If you are a witness for Christ you can testify to the fact that Jesus Christ has saved you and that the Word of God is indeed true.

Worship: This is the act of praising and glorifying God. It is something that God wants us to give to him. Worship can give us joy but it should be more about what it gives to God than what it gives to us.

WHO'S WHO

Jesus Christ: The Son of God, who was sent to this world as a human child within the womb of the virgin Mary. He had no earthly father. He was conceived with the power of the Holy Spirit.

Saul/Paul: At first an extreme Pharisee he persecuted the early church by arresting Christians and throwing them in prison. He was also present at the murder of Stephen though he did not take part. After an encounter with the risen Jesus Christ on the Damascus road Saul became a believer and eventually had his name changed to Paul. Paul became a preacher and evangelist and took the Good News of Salvation to many countries in Southern Europe.

Aquila and Priscilla: Two companions of Paul's who had the same trade as he had – tent making.

Barnabas: One of Paul's travelling companions was Barnabas. His name means Son of Encouragement. After travelling with Paul they eventually fell out and went their separate ways.

Eutychus: A young man who fell from an upper floor window during one of Paul's sermons. Paul brought him back to life, however, and the congregation went back inside to listen to more.

Luke: One of Paul's travelling companions, and the man behind the Gospel of Luke and the Book of Acts. He was a physician by trade.

Silas: Another travelling companion of Paul's who was present with him in the jail at Philippi.

Timothy: A young Christian pastor who had a Jewish mother and a Greek father. He accompanied Paul on some of his journeys. Paul was his mentor.

ROMAN RULERS AT THE TIME OF PAUL

Claudius: The fourth Roman Emperor ruling from A.D. 41 to his death in A.D. 54.

Agrippa: A descendant of Herod the Great. He became governor of Judea at the time of Claudius.

Felix: Governor of Judea A.D. 52-58.

Festus: Governor of Judea from A.D. 58 to 62. The successor of Felix.

THE TRINITY

The Bible shows us one God in three persons not three separate Gods. The Father, Son and Holy Spirit. These three are one God – the same in substance, equal in power and glory.

God the Father: This is the first person of the Trinity. God, the Father, is the one who sent God the Son to this world as the Saviour for sinners. Jesus Christ intercedes for his people before God the Father.

God the Son: He is just like the Father and he was sent by the Father to be our Saviour. He did everything that the Father asked, even going to the cross to carry our sin and guilt. Jesus is in the presence of God, the Father, interceding for us – representing us. Jesus prayed to God the Father often. He prayed to God, the Father, specifically for those people that God the Father had given to him.

God the Holy Spirit: The Holy Spirit helped Jesus with everything that he did. The Holy Spirit makes his home in our hearts when we become Christians. He teaches us, guides us and helps us to become like Jesus. He also helps us to pray to the Father.

OLD TESTAMENT CHARACTERS

Elijah: An Old Testament prophet. Read about him in 1 and 2 Kings.

David: The second king of Israel. You can read about him in 1 and 2 Samuel – also in *40 Days with David*.

Abraham: Old Testament prophet (Genesis 20:7). The father of Isaac, grandfather of Jacob and Esau; great grandfather of Joseph and his brothers. Read about him in Genesis chapters 12-25.

BOOT CAMP: 001 – GETTING STARTED WITH YOU.

 WHO ARE YOU? When asked that question you'll give your name. You might add something about where you are from and what you do. Someone else has different answers. There is nobody else exactly like you. However, there are things that everybody has in common.

1. We are all human beings. God created us.

CREATED BY GOD. This means made by God. God is our Creator. He made the world. The universe and everything that exists in it is his creation.

2. We all sin. We disobey God.

SIN. This is disobedience to God's instructions in thoughts words or deeds. If we do not listen to or obey God then we don't love him. That is sin.

3. Sin deserves God's punishment.

PUNISHMENT. The punishment for sin is death – eternal death in hell. So sin is a big problem for all of us.

Sin is failing to match the perfect standard God has set. You may think that you aren't that bad. But the Bible tells us that the soul that sins shall die and that all have sinned. We cannot get to heaven on our own. God's Word tells us that if we trust in Jesus Christ we will be given eternal life. Remember that 'the wages of sin is death but the gift of God is eternal life through Jesus Christ his Son' (Romans 6:23).

HEAVEN. This is one of the places that you can go to when you die. You can only go there if you love and trust in Jesus Christ. Heaven is perfect in every way because it is where God is. There is no sin there.

HELL. Those who do not turn away from sin to follow Christ go to hell when they die. Just as heaven is for ever so is hell.

THE DEVIL. He is in conflict with God. He tempted the first human beings. Sin, death and the devil have been defeated by Jesus Christ and his death on the cross.

Remember that 'the wages of sin is death but the gift of God is eternal life'. Does the fact that God is willing to give you a gift make you wonder about what God is like? Let's find out!

BOOT CAMP: 002 – GETTING STARTED WITH GOD.

 WHO IS GOD AND WHAT IS HE LIKE? Have you ever tried to describe someone when they are not there? You might describe their appearance, their likes and dislikes, how they behave, what they do. But a verbal description doesn't really show what your friend is like. To know what someone is really like you have to meet them for yourself.

Describing what God is like is difficult too. You can't see God because he is a Spirit; he doesn't have a body. Jesus Christ, also known as God the Son, does have a body. Jesus was on earth for a while, but is now in heaven. We can't physically see God the Father. We can't see God the Son either – at least not yet. So how can we know God for ourselves? What is he like? The Bible tells us some things:

1. God is faithful. Deuteronomy 7:9

2. God is love. Romans 5:8

3. God is just or fair. Psalm 9:16

There are many other things that we can find out about God in his Word, The Bible.

GOD'S WORD. This is also called the Bible. It was written by different people but each of them was told what to write by God. There are two sections – the Old Testament and the New Testament. The Old Testament teaches us about what God did before Jesus came to earth and then the New Testament teaches us about the life of Jesus and what happened after his death and resurrection.

BOOT CAMP: 003 – INTRODUCING JESUS.

 GETTING TO KNOW CHRIST! To really know someone you have to meet them and get to know them personally. You have to love them and be close to them. It is the same with God. And the only way we can really get to know God is through Jesus Christ, his Son. Jesus came to earth to bring people back to God.

CHRISTMAS. Read the REAL Christmas story for yourself in Matthew chapters 1–2; and Luke chapters 1–2.

Jesus was born as a baby. So he was fully human and fully God. But though he was human like us he was sinless. Because he was sinless he was the only one who could take God's punishment for sin. This is what happened when he died on the cross. Because Jesus took this punishment due for the sins of his people, from God his Father, sinners can be saved from sin. When you trust in Jesus Christ, when you believe that he has taken the punishment for your sin, when you turn from your sin and give your love to God you will be saved.

AUTHORITY. Jesus Christ has all power and authority. This has been given to him by God the Father. He has authority over creation, sickness and disease. He even has authority over death and sin. He can forgive sins. He conquered sin, death and the devil on the cross. His authority and control is over all things. The devil can do nothing that is outside God's control. Jesus Christ has authority over you and me. There is nothing that can separate us from his love when we trust in him. There are no leaders or powers that can thwart his plans or purposes.

BOOT CAMP: 003 – Introducing Jesus.

CRUCIFIXION. This was the method of execution that the Romans used at the time of the occupation of Palestine. It is the method they used to kill Jesus. A cross was made out of wood, onto which a criminal was nailed. The cross was erected and the criminal was then left to hang there until he died. The Jewish religious leaders falsely accused Jesus of many things and then handed him over to the Roman authorities. Pilate, the Roman governor, made a weak attempt to free Jesus but in the end he agreed to crucify him.

Note that there is more to Christ's crucifixion than a murder. Jesus had to die in order to save people from their sins. The punishment for sin had to be paid, otherwise sinners would have to bear it themselves and would not be allowed into heaven. So, although this crucifixion is a dreadful event, it is also the one event that brings sinners back to God.

RESURRECTION. The resurrection is what happened three days after the death of Jesus Christ. He was raised to life again. This shows that he had accomplished everything he had come to do. He had defeated the power of sin and death. His body was raised from the dead by God (Acts 2:24). All who trust in Christ will be raised to life again too, with bodies that will last forever. In these bodies we will be with Jesus for all eternity – sinless, holy and praising God.

ASCENSION. After the resurrection Jesus was seen by many people. After he had promised the disciples the gift of the Holy Spirit, Jesus went back to heaven. He ascended to heaven in a cloud. Right now he is in the presence of God the Father and he is interceding for his people. Interceding means that Jesus is appearing in the presence of God on our behalf (Hebrews 9:12, 24). He is there as our sacrifice for sin. He is our advocate and representative and through him we have access to God, the Father.

 CREATION (GENESIS 1–3). God created the world and human kind. He created everything perfectly. There was no sin. On Day 7 of creation God rested, not because he was tired, but because he was starting something special: A day of rest for mankind – the Sabbath, or the Lord's Day. The first man and woman, Adam and Eve, lived in the Garden of Eden. In the Garden there were lots of fruit trees. But there was one tree that God instructed Adam and Eve not to eat from. This was the tree of the knowledge of good and evil.

THE FALL (GENESIS 3). The devil, in the guise of a serpent, deceived Eve into eating the forbidden fruit. She ate it and then gave some to Adam. He ate it too. They disobeyed and sin entered the world. The world was spoiled, as was Adam and Eve's relationship with God. God had to banish them from the Garden, but there was a special promise that he made. He promised to send a rescuer. One of Eve's descendants would finally destroy the devil who had caused such harm. This descendant was Jesus Christ, the Son of God himself.

BOOT CAMP: 005 – The Old Testament.

THE OLD TESTAMENT. The account of Creation and the Fall is at the beginning of the Bible in the Old Testament. Other incidents follow which explain what happened from then on. After the flood (Genesis 6–8), we read about the sons of Noah and the people who came after that. Abraham and Sarah were chosen by God to begin a new nation called the Israelites. God promised Abraham and his descendants that they would have a land of their own. Abraham's son was named Isaac, and his son was named Jacob. Jacob had twelve sons, one of whom was Joseph. Joseph's brothers sold him as a slave to Egypt. Eventually he was helped by God and rose to a high position in the land of Egypt. He was used by God to save the lives of the very brothers who had sold him into slavery. His older brother, Judah, is the one, however, who features in the family tree of the Lord Jesus.

THE EXODUS (BOOK OF EXODUS). The Israelites' stay in Egypt did not work out well in the end. A new Pharaoh was crowned and he did not like the Israelite people. This Pharaoh enslaved the Israelites and they were treated harshly. He even attempted to kill all the Israelite baby boys. One, however, escaped and was rescued and brought up by Pharaoh's daughter. His name was Moses. In the end God told Moses to lead his people out of Egypt to the land that he had promised them. Pharaoh would not agree to this. God sent plagues on the Egyptians. It was not until the tenth terrible plague that Pharaoh agreed to let God's people go.

PASSOVER OR FEAST OF UNLEAVENED BREAD.

The Passover was a feast that the Israelites celebrated in honour of the day that God released them from the

BOOT CAMP: 005 – THE OLD TESTAMENT.

 Egyptians. The Israelites were told to have a special feast of lamb and bitter herbs and flat bread. They were to be ready to leave their homes at a moment's notice. All the Israelites had to sacrifice a lamb. The blood of the lamb was to go on the doorposts of their houses and on the lintels. The Lord would pass over these houses and not touch any who were inside. However, the Lord visited the Egyptians. The first-born in every family died. When the Lord passed over the houses of the Israelites this was a wonderful time for them – they had been saved. God instructed them to remember this special day by having a celebration every year.

The Israelites left for the Promised Land. It took them many years but God looked after them. Eventually the descendants of Abraham made it to the land God had promised.

THE TEN COMMANDMENTS. When the Israelites travelled to the Promised Land God instructed them how to live. He gave ten specific instructions called the Ten Commandments. These were written by God himself into two tablets of stone and given to Moses. Read about this in Exodus 20.

Bible Book Summary:

ACTS

This book is addressed to Theophilus. However nothing is known about this character. The book itself is written by Luke, the physician. Acts records the early history of the Christian Church. It begins with the Ascension of Jesus to heaven and then it follows the growth of Christianity as it spreads from Palestine, throughout Asia and eventually to Rome. Peter is the prominent character in the first few chapters. However, the greater part of the book is taken up with Paul and his companions during their missionary journeys.

ROMANS

This letter appears first in the Bible but is not the first of Paul's Epistles. It was written to Christians at Rome whom Paul hoped to visit. In this book Paul gives strong teaching about the Christian faith, covering amongst other issues the topics of sin, law and salvation. The letter closes with spiritual advice and some personal remarks.

I CORINTHIANS

This letter discusses various problems that faced the Corinthian church at that time. Writing from Ephesus Paul addressed the Corinthian church regarding the importance of their new life in Christ, fellowship within the Church, spiritual gifts, Christian love and the meaning of the Resurrection.

II CORINTHIANS

II Corinthians is a very personal letter and tells of the many difficulties and hardships Paul endured as he laboured for the kingdom of God.

GALATIANS

This letter was addressed to the churches in Galatia and one of its great themes is that of Christian freedom. In it Paul attacks the Christians who wished to exalt the law. There is a great focus on doctrine but this is followed by practical teachings too.

EPHESIANS

This is one of the letters that Paul wrote from prison – the other letters being Philippians, Colossians, and Philemon. Here Paul discusses the believers' exalted position in Christ, the Church as the body of Christ, her relationship to God, and how the Gospel impacts our lives.

PHILIPPIANS

This letter is really a message of joy; Paul expresses thankfulness for the Philippians' love and help. The epistle presents the humility of Jesus in a wonderful way and gives some wonderful practical advice to people facing day to day problems such as Euodia and Syntyche.

COLOSSIANS

This is a brief letter that is well known for its doctrine. In it Paul insists upon the Lordship of Christ.

I AND II THESSALONIANS

These two letters are probably the earliest writings of Paul. Written in A.D. 51-52, soon after the founding of the Thessalonian church, Paul is helping to sort out some basic problems facing the church in Thessalonica. Paul particularly teaches about what is going to happen before and during the return of Christ.

I AND II TIMOTHY

This is one of the 'pastoral epistles'. The letters to Timothy discuss the duties and qualifications of church officers, the inspiration of Scripture, the treatment of widows, and the prospect of a reward in the future.

TITUS

This is another pastoral and personal letter written by Paul to a young minister in Crete. The letter to Titus is practical and discusses the day to day problems faced by a young minister.

PHILEMON

This is the shortest of Paul's letters and again was a personal one addressed to a man named Philemon. Paul's letter is written with the hope that Philemon, the master of a runaway slave named Onesimus, will receive the young man back as a brother in Christ.

HEBREWS

There is some debate as to who wrote this epistle. It may have been written by Paul so we shall include it here. It portrays Jesus, who was the perfect sacrifice for the sins of the world, as the great High Priest. Hebrews chapter 11 includes the Bible's only definition of faith and then goes onto present a great list of men and women of faith.

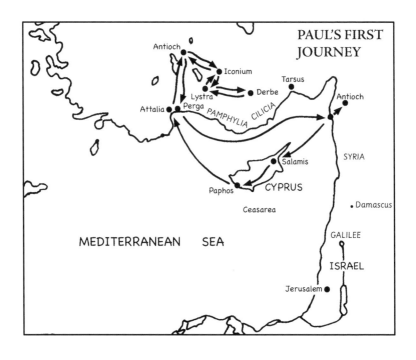

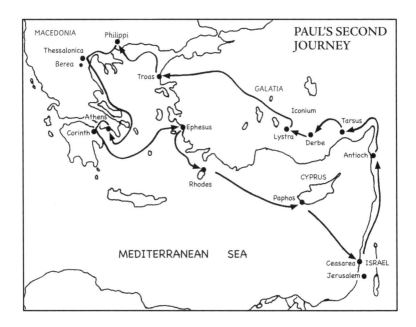

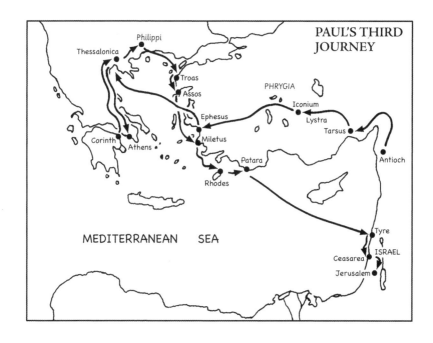

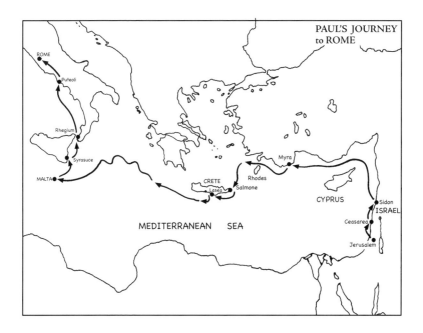

CHRISTIAN FOCUS PUBLICATIONS

Christian Focus · Christian Heritage · CF4K · Mentor

Christian Focus Publications publishes books for adults and children under its four main imprints: Christian Focus, Christian Heritage, CF4K and Mentor. Our books reflect that God's word is reliable and Jesus is the way to know him, and live for ever with him.

Our children's publication list includes a Sunday school curriculum that covers pre-school to early teens; puzzle and activity books. We also publish personal and family devotional titles, biographies and inspirational stories that children will love.

If you are looking for quality Bible teaching for children then we have an excellent range of Bible story and age specific theological books.

From pre-school to teenage fiction, we have it covered!

**Find us at our web page:
www.christianfocus.com**

BLYTHSWOOD CARE

Blythswood Care is a Christian charity involved in care projects in south east Europe, in international aid and in the distribution of Christian literature. Since 2002, Blythswood Care has cooperated with Christian Focus Publications in the production of children's books in several European languages.

**Find us at our webpage:
www.blythswood.org**